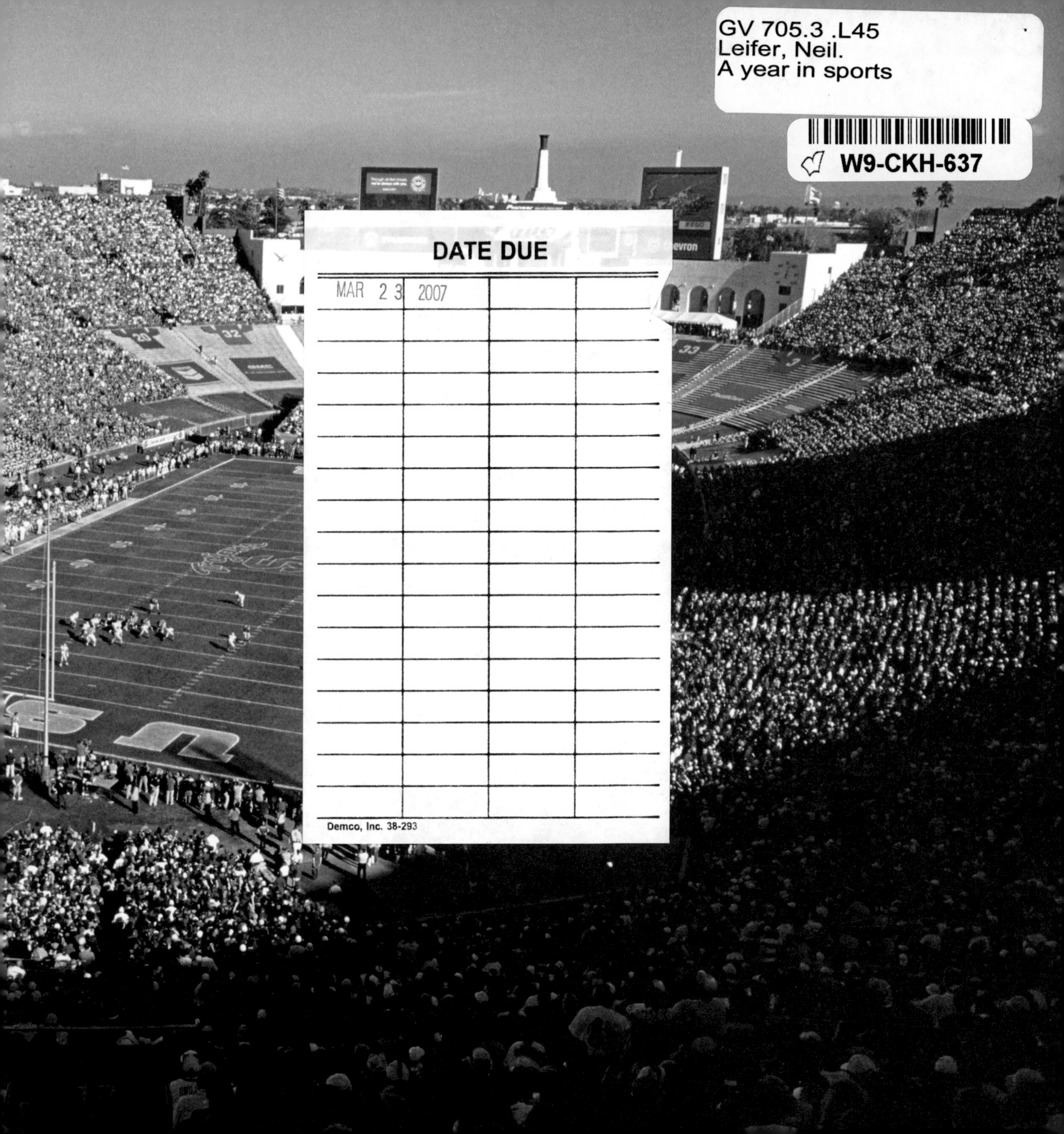

SPORTS

A YEAR IN

FROM THE ROSE BOWL TO FIGURE SKATING

NEIL LEIFER

INTRODUCTION BY
FRANK DEFORD

ABBEVILLE PRESS PUBLISHERS
NEW YORK LONDON

FRONT COVER:
PATRIOTS QUARTERBACK TOM BRADY
SUPER BOWL XXXIX, EAGLES VS. PATRIOTS
JACKSONVILLE, FLORIDA
FEBRUARY 6, 2005

BACK COVER:
THE HEAT'S SHAQUILLE O'NEAL
MIAMI HEAT VS. DETROIT PISTONS
NBA PLAYOFFS
MIAMI, FLORIDA
JUNE 2, 2005

PAGES 2–3:
TIGER WOODS
THE BRITISH OPEN, ST. ANDREWS, SCOTLAND
JULY 17, 2005

PAGE 12:
MUHAMMAD ALI VS. CLEVELAND
WILLIAMS
HOUSTON ASTRODOME, HOUSTON, TEXAS
NOVEMBER 14, 1966

EDITOR: Susan Costello
DESIGNER: Patricia Fabricant
TEXT EDITOR: Steven Cannella
PICTURE EDITOR: Howie Leifer
ASSISTANT TO NEIL LEIFER: Joan Fazekas
PRODUCTION MANAGER: Louise Kurtz

SI Covers reprinted with permission from
SPORTS ILLUSTRATED © 2006
PAGES 218–19: Photograph of the National
Tennis Center from the MetLife Blimp.
PAGES 234–39: Photographs of Yankee Stadium
from the FUJIFILM BLIMP.

First edition
10 9 8 7 6 5 4 3 2 1

ISBN 13: 978-0-7892-0903-0
ISBN 10: 0-7892-0903-9

Library of Congress Cataloging-in-Publication Data
Leifer, Neil.
  A year in sports / photography and text by Neil
Leifer ; introduction by
Frank Deford. — 1st ed.
     p. cm.
  Includes bibliographical references and index.
  ISBN-13: 978-0-7892-0903-0 (alk. paper)
  1. Sports—Pictorial works. 2. Athletes—Pictorial
works. I. Title.

GV705.3.L45 2006
796.022'2—DC22

2006011314

For bulk and premium sales and for text adoption
procedures, write to Customer Service Manager,
Abbeville Press, 137 Varick Street, New York, NY
10013 or call 1-800-ARTBOOK

FOR TERRY McDONELL, FRANK DEFORD, AND COREY LEIFER

CONTENTS

PREFACE

On December 18, 2005, I watched the San Diego Chargers defeat the Indianapolis Colts at the RCA Dome in Indianapolis. For the Colts, it was like being jolted from a beautiful dream. They had entered the game with a perfect 13–0 record, and the Chargers had dashed their hopes of being the first undefeated National Football League team since the 1972 Miami Dolphins. For the Colts, something special had ended. I KNEW EXACTLY HOW THEY FELT, because the game also marked the end of a story-book year for me: It was the last stop on a fantastic journey that I had dubbed the Neil Leifer Senior Citizen Tour. The Tour was my return to sports photography after a 26-year hiatus, and the experience was even more thrilling than I had anticipated. Beginning on New Year's Day, when I shot the Rose Bowl, I lived a fan's fantasy for 12 months. The Super Bowl, the Final Four, the Masters, the Kentucky Derby, the Tour de France, the World Series—if it was on the front page of the sports pages, I was there, and I had the best seat in the house. All the old sports metaphors applied: I had gone undefeated and batted a thousand. Well, almost—I did miss a few shots I wish I had gotten. But as I flew home to New York from Indianapolis, I was proud to have taken some wonderful pictures. I was exhilarated that the Tour had worked out so well. And I was sad that it was over. Like the Colts, I too was waking up from a beautiful dream. I GREW UP ON THE SIDELINES and in the photo pens of the world's great sports venues. I was 16 when *Sports Illustrated* first started to notice my pictures in 1959. Soon after I was working for the magazine, and for the next two decades I traveled the world with my *SI* credential as my passport. By the time I left *SI* in February 1978 for a job at *Time* magazine I had shot 17 Kentucky Derbies, 15 Masters golf tournaments, 7 Olympics, more than 100 World Series games, and 21 National Football League championship games, including the first 12 Super Bowls. It was a wonderful ride, but I was ready for new challenges. At *Time* I had the occasional sports assignment, but I never thought I'd see another Super Bowl, Masters, or Kentucky Derby in person. I was still a fan—to this day I read the sports pages first—but I didn't miss my life in sports. I really had no interest in going to any major sporting events. How could I? For 20 years I had been on the sidelines for Super Bowls, next to the dugout for World Series, and on the apron at title fights. There was no way I could see things simply as a fan the way I had from behind the lens. I started thinking about sports again in 2002, when Terry McDonell became managing editor of *Sports Illustrated*. We were casual friends, and I'd always been a fan of Terry's work. He liked mine, too. He put a shot I took of Johnny Unitas on *SI*'s cover when the great quarterback died in 2002. And I was really happy when he used a picture I took at the first Super Bowl on the cover in 2004. I thought both covers looked great, and once in a while, when we'd get together for dinner, Terry would suggest that I should shoot something new for *SI*. While I was intrigued, I hadn't seriously shot a sports picture in more than 25 years. I told Terry it's not something you just jump back into. More importantly, I knew that I didn't have the passion for sports photography that I did when I was young. And passion, I've always known, was what made me a good photographer. If I was going to do something, I wanted to do it right. I was afraid

I would embarrass Terry and myself by not living up to my old standards. BUT I HAD TO ADMIT I was very flattered that Terry had asked me to be in the magazine, so I started kicking around ideas. In the spring of 2004 I had a brainstorm. What if I spent a year covering the events that were such an important part of my youth? I could show how sports and photography have evolved, and provide a personal, unique look at our marquee sports events. I even had a name in mind. I love going to the movies, and four days before the 2005 Rose Bowl I would turn 62, the age at which New Yorkers are eligible for senior citizen ticket discounts. I was about to become a senior citizen, so why not call my project exactly what it was: the Senior Citizen Tour. I WAS ECSTATIC when Terry said he liked the idea. (I mentioned the project to Ross Greenberg, the president of HBO Sports, and he said he wanted to do a piece on me and the Tour for the show *Real Sports with Bryant Gumbel*. The segment ran on HBO in November 2005.) Terry had given me a ticket to sports heaven, the equivalent of a toy store awarding a lucky kid a yearlong shop-for-free card. By the time I started the Tour the old passion was back, and I was as excited as I had been for any assignment in the 1960s and '70s. They say you can't go home again, but I did—and I had a terrific time. FROM DAY ONE IT WAS A BLAST, and because I wasn't responsible for news coverage I could go for things like aerials of Yankee Stadium, not caring that the Yankees and Red Sox were fighting for a division title 1,500 feet below me. The Tour was my chance to focus on subjects I found intriguing, even if they hadn't scored the winning touchdown or thrown a knockout punch. I could get an insider's look at what it's like when the president of the United

States throws out the first pitch on Opening Day. I could concentrate on sports beauty with subjects like Maria Sharapova and the Dallas Cowboys Cheerleaders. People always ask me if I ever worked on the Swimsuit Issue for *Sports Illustrated*. The answer's no, but I can say I finally got to shoot some of the most striking women in sports. SPORTS, AND PHOTOGRAPHY, had changed big time while I was gone. With so many first-rate shooters at all the major events today, it's that much tougher to find a unique shot. The technology is better, too. Steve Fine, *SI*'s director of photography, insisted that I shoot digitally all year, a suggestion I strongly resisted. But with the help of David Bergman, an *SI* photographer and my digital tutor, by June I came to realize that the new technology is far superior to shooting on film. For the last six months of the project I shot 100 percent digital. And, Steve and David will be happy to know that, at the end of the year, I bought my first digital camera for personal use. I HAD SUCH A GOOD TIME that after that Colts game I made a promise to myself: I'm going on another excursion when I'm 75. (Whoever the managing editor of *SI* is then should expect a call in 2017.) I'll call it the Really Senior Citizen Tour. I can't wait.

—NEIL LEIFER

INTRODUCTION

IT SURPRISES PEOPLE TO LEARN that writers and photographers don't work much together. In all my years at *Sports Illustrated* and other magazines, I can't remember traveling with a photographer more than three or four times. Nothing personal, you understand, although to be perfectly honest, the truth is I don't want a photographer around when I'm doing a story. That's simply because when a photographer is there, most all anybody cares about is looking good for the camera—and not, by process of elimination, talking to yours truly. IN PARTICULAR, athletes like photographers more than writers. Wouldn't you? Photographers take your pretty picture. Writers might just very well write something nasty about you. ON THE OTHER HAND, we writers are more celebrated. We get bylines. We even get our names on the cover of a magazine, when the photographer who took the very picture that is the cover, might end up with a citation for that tucked away at the bottom of an index page that nobody reads. Often as not, photographer credits are written out in tiny agate type *vertically* next to their pictures—very possibly even uncomfortably stuck next to the staples. Now, that's really unfair. OF COURSE, YOU'VE GOT TO UNDERSTAND that there's a good reason for this, human-nature-wise. Editors were writers. (Most of them weren't very good writers, which is why they became editors—but that's another story.) So ex-writers are more inclined to boost their own brethren, while slighting the shooters. Also, writers tend to think of themselves as *artistes*, while photographers are perceived as mere technicians, button-pushers, who basically have only three words in their vocabulary. These are: "Just one more."

(And of course, they're lying anyhow. *Just one more*, my foot.)

Therefore, it is with a certain amount of justice and fair play (and even a little guilt) that I am delighted to pay respects here to Neil Leifer. He is one of the very best photographers of our time. Maybe, in fact, Neil is the very best. Certainly, he is the most creative, and his oeuvre deserves all the respect that we writers lavish on ourselves. Neil is an artist, and this lovely book with his most recent work shows that truth so magnificently once again.

This year-full of his sports pictures was occasioned by Neil's sixty-second birthday, which officially made him "a senior citizen." Neil had left *Sports Illustrated* in 1978. Not since then had he shot such events as the World Series and Super Bowl, the Kentucky Derby, and the Masters—championships he had photographed year after year for almost two decades. So here was a chance for him to go back in time, the best anyone could, and shoot many of the same events that he had documented in the past. Terry McDonell, the managing editor of *Sports Illustrated,* approved the concept for the magazine, and Leifer himself further envisioned the whole book that you've already carefully looked through. (You see, just as people being photographed pay no attention to writers, so

too do people who buy books of photography pay no attention to the words in the books until they've devotedly studied all the pictures.)

Shooting in 2005, however, Leifer had much more freedom than when he first worked these games back in his salad days. Then, he had to concentrate on the action, looking for the most important shots that related to the game result. Now, though, he could altogether forget the quarterback or the knockout or the play at home plate and seek out more imaginative views. This flexibility excited him because, curiously, despite all the success Leifer enjoyed shooting game action in a variety of sports, he never thought that was his forte. Now he could play strictly to his strengths.

Just as so many sports demand superior hand-eye coordination, so too does the shooter covering those sports with the long lenses that are so common to sports photography, require the same split-second abilities. Position matters a great deal, of course, but even when a photographer is in the right place to capture a play, he must be able to close the deal in that perfect instant.

Leifer always believed that his contemporary, friend and rival, Walter Iooss, possessed superior natural ability. Even now, he unabashedly calls Iooss a "genius." But in compensation, Leifer possessed the better—often even unique—concepts. Before the first Super Bowl in Los Angeles in 1967, for example, Leifer took up a position high in the Coliseum and shot the pre-game coin toss, showing the two co-captains of the Packers and the Chiefs and the referee alone in the middle of the great gridiron. Walter Iooss laughs: "Now, who the hell would shoot a coin toss?"

Indeed, the picture was meaningless at the time, but over the years, as the ceremony became more crowded and more of a production number, that original intimate little session began to take on a wonderful, quaint, period quality. Two years ago, McDonell, the *SI* editor, was looking for a photograph to put on the cover of a special Super Bowl reprise issue. He idly mentioned his quest one night when he was dining at Elaine's, the famous Manhattan restaurant. Elaine Kaufman, the alert proprietor, immediately hied to a different part of the premises, took down Leifer's coin-toss photo from the wall there, and presented it to McDonell. "Here's your cover," she said.

And sure enough, it was.

This past year, when Leifer returned to shoot the Super Bowl in Jacksonville, he naturally shot the coin toss from the same vantage as he had thirty-nine years ago, and presto: two pictures are worth a thousand words. Nothing can illustrate the bloated growth of the Super Bowl as well as these simple paired pictures. *Now, who the hell would shoot a coin toss?*

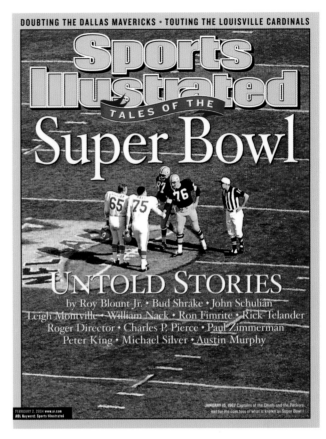

SPORTS ILLUSTRATED COVER
SUPER BOWL XXXVIII
FEBRUARY 2, 2004

If Leifer believes that he must devote himself to preparation in order to gain the right shot, his most outstanding innate artistic quality surely involves his sense of composition. Laughing, Iooss even swears that Leifer was able to take shots that not only caught the action perfectly, but which neatly allowed for the magazine's logo at the top of the frame. Be that as it may, Leifer's sense of composition has been crucial to his success. Look at his simple pictures of stadiums. Compare what he does with four disparate structures: Yankee Stadium—baseball; Arthur Ashe Stadium—tennis; Churchill Downs—horse racing; Franklin Field—track and field. Each image employs the huge edifice in a different way; each makes the stadium a different character in his picture play.

Especially since the auto-focus telephoto lenses have made it so much easier for photographers to come in close to the action and still get dead-sharp images—up close and personal!—shooters can easily be seduced by that expressive, sometimes even violent, intimacy. Leifer often manages to capture the spirit of the occasion better by going in the other direction, working against type, keeping the athletes in miniature, embracing the whole, evocative scene with his camera. I think this is particularly valuable now that television so prefers tight shots. How sweetly are both Tiger Woods (in his triumph) and Jack Nicklaus (in his valedictory)

caught at the British Open with the magnificent old St. Andrews clubhouse looming beyond them.

When Leifer was a boy in New York, delivering sandwiches after school for the Stage Deli in midtown Manhattan, he would struggle for the chance to get credentials for sporting events. Sometimes he could do nothing but purchase student discount seats, shooting down on flyspeck players from the distant reaches of Yankee Stadium or Madison Square Garden. Sometimes he had better luck trundling off to Philadelphia or Baltimore, where the team PR chiefs were more generous than their hardened Noo Yawk counterparts. (He'd take the bus to Philly for $6, instead of the eight-buck train ride, using the savings to buy a couple more precious, expensive rolls of film.)

For the football Giants games, Leifer found a particularly clever dodge. There, at Yankee Stadium, he would volunteer to push the disabled veterans in wheelchairs, who were allowed to watch the game from the field, lined up just behind the end zone. Safely inside, Neil would then bring coffee over to the sideline security guards, who would thus be more inclined to look the other way when the young wheelchair escort would bring out his cheap camera and surreptitiously start shooting action from the sidelines.

So it was that, on his sixteenth birthday, Leifer was standing behind the end zone in the gloaming

JACK NICKLAUS
THE BRITISH OPEN, ST. ANDREWS, SCOTLAND
JULY 15, 2005

ALAN AMECHE TOUCHDOWN
New York Giants vs. Baltimore Colts, NFL Championship Game
Yankee Stadium, Bronx, New York
December 28, 1958

INTRODUCTION

of that fabled December Sunday in 1958, when Johnny Unitas led the Baltimore Colts to victory in overtime over the Giants in what would be called "the greatest football game ever played." The winning touchdown came when Unitas handed off to Alan Ameche, who bulled in over right tackle. Leifer's picture—among the very first of his to appear in print—does show Ameche scoring, but because Leifer was using only a basic, inexpensive camera, he could not zero in on the fullback the way any sensible, veteran photographer would. Instead, he was forced to take in the whole scene—Unitas looking on from where he'd handed off, the lights of the stadium beaming down, the wintry sky above.

It was less than two years later (although he was still only seventeen), that Leifer was an accredited pro, shooting the Yankees–Pirates World Series at Forbes Field. He had his first fancy camera, a $450 number bought on the installment plan, and it was he—not some *Sports Illustrated* regular—who took the one picture that the magazine could run in color in that first issue of the Series: a shot of Yogi Berra being caught off second, tagged by Bill Mazeroski (see page 20). Together with another black-and-white shot, he earned just enough to pay for his new camera outright. He was walking on air. "This," he says, "was the moment I realized I could hold my own shooting against the big boys."

Then, in the seventh game, when Mazeroski hit his home run to win the Series, Leifer was right on him as he swung away. But a terrific older photographer, Marvin Newman, was positioned near Leifer, and he eschewed the obvious. Newman shot the whole scene, the scoreboard, the players watching as Mazeroski, down in the corner of the frame, made history. That became the classic image of that arresting moment, just as Leifer's wider shot of Ameche scoring better caught that climactic instant. Leifer never forgot: yes, sometimes less close can be more, primitive can be better.

In terms of planned composition, though, Leifer's masterpiece is perhaps his simplest, with his symmetry at its most obvious. He placed a camera directly above the ring in the Astrodome the night Muhammad Ali fought one Cleveland Williams in 1966. When Ali knocked out Williams, there it was: the square shot embracing the squared ring within—the stark white canvas, with only the champion and referee standing upon it, the loser's limp body spread-eagled near one corner.

It was this picture that *The Observer* chose as the greatest sports photograph ever taken. Leifer, too, knows that no one can ever satisfactorily duplicate it, because much of the frame is so pure and clean, so pearly white, whereas all boxing canvasses today are cluttered with large lettering and bright logos identifying the arena and a sponsor or two.

YOGI BERRA AND BILL MAZEROSKI (#9)
WORLD SERIES GAME 1, FORBES FIELD,
PITTSBURGH, PENNSYLVANIA
OCTOBER 6, 1960

INTRODUCTION

Leifer also believes that the gritty hue that boxing pictures had in the past will never be quite as dramatic again. There's a simple reason for this that has nothing to do with the advance of film technology. Rather, it used to be common in arenas for smoking to be allowed. By the time of the main event, the cigarette and cigar smoke had permeated the whole atmosphere in a building, so that photographs appeared to be shot through some sort of haze. The hanging smoke even gave color photographs a special bluish tint. Fans' lungs may be clearer now, and so too boxing photographs, but the old shots had a visual ambience that's missing today.

If Leifer carefully conceived the symmetrical Astrodome boxing photograph, by far his most famous shot (and number two on *The Observer*'s all-time list) the outcome was not only unplanned, but the product of the most fortuitous circumstance. (Leifer is the first to acknowledge that luck can play a large role in sports photography. Positions are usually assigned. So as good as you might be, if the quarterback throws the touchdown to the other side of the field, all the instinct and technique in the world are for naught. But Leifer also makes this wry observation: "It's amazing how often the best photographers are the ones who get lucky.")

Anyway, on the night Ali defended his title against Sonny Liston in a little hockey arena in Lewiston, Maine, Leifer and the other *Sports Illustrated* photographer, Herb Scharfman, were given positions on opposite sides of the ring. When Ali knocked Liston out in the first round, he fell directly before Leifer, anchoring a scene that Leifer could not have better choreographed. Liston's arm did not cover his face. Then Ali stood right above his downed opponent—dead-on before Leifer—scowling. And then, in a flash, Ali waved one hand across his body, taunting Liston. The gesture is frozen forever in Leifer's shot. It was but for an instant, and Leifer trapped the nanosecond perfectly. More luck: the referee was just far enough away to be out of the shot, leaving the picture perfectly framed, as if it were posed. There is only the victor and the vanquished midst the hazy blue light—and, of course, as the fillip, poor Scharfman, the other *SI* photographer, looks on desperately at the rear of the action, right smack between Ali's legs.

Leifer made the trip back to little Lewiston as part of his 2005 travels. The good city fathers were so honored that the man who made the great photograph there was returning that they put a ring back in the arena, surrounding it with rows of chairs, exactly as the scene was set forty years ago on the night the place was filled and famous. This time, Leifer made sure to take a self-portrait of himself in the ring—and so too did the local newspaper, putting a picture of the photographer on page one, standing where he had shot Ali so long ago.

Ali has been, of course, Leifer's favorite subject, and it is only natural that he would also capture the old champ himself, now relaxed and at peace—and, with the two of them, together, holding that famous Lewiston photograph. Also, of course, Leifer shot Ali's daughter, Laila, for women box now, and she is a champion, too.

When I think of Leifer and Ali, though, I especially remember a time when I was with them a few years ago in Washington. Leifer wanted to

OPPOSITE:
MUHAMMAD ALI VS. SONNY LISTON
ST. DOMINICK'S ARENA, LEWISTON, MAINE
MAY 25, 1965

ABOVE
HOWARD BINGHAM AND MUHAMMAD ALI
THE VIETNAM MEMORIAL, WASHINGTON, D.C.
MAY 1998

pose Ali by the Vietnam Memorial. Now I considered this to be an absolutely mad idea. After all, apart only, possibly, from Jane Fonda, no one person was more identified in opposition to the war than was Ali.

But Neil thought that at least since Ali had lit the flame at the Atlanta Olympics in '96, the enmity against him had faded, so off we went to the monument. It was a gloomy, gray day, but a number of people were already gathered in the shelter of that wonderful, reflective wall. Most of them seemed to be women, and they were tracing their hands along the wall, searching for the names of the father or the brother or the lover or the husband who had been killed in the war Ali would not fight.

Neil posed Ali by the wall alone, and then with his good friend and personal photographer, Howard Bingham. He was shooting away when I saw the first visitors there notice who it was who was being photographed. They began to move in our direction. Oh, my, I thought, now we're going to have a terrible confrontation. But no; instead, when the women realized it was Ali, they rushed to him, called out happily to him, shook his hand, even handed me their little cameras so that I might take a picture of them standing there before the wall with the old champ.

I thought to myself then: well, the Vietnam War must truly be over at last.

LEIFER OOZES THE TRADITIONS of his profession. He venerates the superb news and sports photographers who came before him, and collects their work. Almost all he knew personally. Leifer grew up when *LIFE* magazine was what television is now, that window upon the world that you could view from your living room, and as a boy he was able to connect personally with his idols, delivering sandwiches to the *LIFE* studio from the Stage Deli a few blocks away.

Young Neil was blessed with freckles and flaming red hair then, and with this cherubic aspect, he appeared even younger than he was. Indeed, Leifer's youthful countenance made it all the more remarkable that he could burst onto the scene as such a prodigy. The old-line New York newspaper sports photographers gave him no quarter, even actually tried at times to prevent him from working.

However short and callow Leifer was, though, he was never bashful, and he held his own. When he was still the deli delivery boy, he would tell the bemused *LIFE* photographers that someday he would be shooting for *LIFE* or *Sports Illustrated* alongside them. Perhaps, then, the photograph in his collection which means the most to him is the famous *LIFE* magazine shot by Ralph Morse of Jackie Robinson dashing down the third-base line. The inscription reads: "Red—Stage Deli's delivery boy who haunted the Life studio—'You'll see, I'll make it.' You sure did. Ralph Morse."

That picture of Robinson, along with those taken by many other famous *LIFE* photographers—Margaret Bourke-White, Alfred Eisenstadt, Dmitri Kessel, Carl Mydans, Gordon Parks, George Silk—are his dearest possessions. It is revealing that Leifer did not necessarily seek their most famous photos for his collection, but "the ones I remembered and liked best when I was a kid." Likewise, he collects work of his fellow *Sports Illustrated* photographers—a panorama of photos from men such as Jerry Cooke, Mark Kaufman, Marvin Newman, Hy Peskin, John Zimmerman, and of course, Walter Iooss: "Hey," he says, "these were—and still are—my heroes"— even though, as a teenager, he was already holding his own against them.

Leifer is genuinely complimentary of what he learned from these older colleagues. For instance, notwithstanding the world acclaim that his Ali-Liston, Ali-Williams pictures have received, he says this of a photograph of the middleweight Carmen Basilio that was taken by Hy Peskin: "If Carmen Basilio had become Muhammad Ali, nobody would be talking about my Ali pictures."

Yet for all the praise, even awe, he extends to other photographers, Leifer soon developed the utmost confidence in himself. From the time in 1962, when he first saw a photograph Iooss took of the Baltimore Colts' Jimmy Orr catching a pass, he realized that he was up against a superior natural talent. "But I'll tell you," he says, "still, there wasn't a game I shot with Walter that I didn't go in there thinking I would beat him."

It was not, however, a *LIFE* photographer who first captivated Leifer. Rather, it was the star shooter for *Sport*, a fanzine monthly that predated *Sports Illustrated*. The photographer's name was Ozzie Sweet. His pictures, especially of baseball players, were period classics. They were, well, sweet—perfectly lit, wonderfully staged, showing, say, Jackie Robinson pivoting over the bag at second on the double play. The portraits did not depict athletes so much as idealized young gods, the look of eagles upon all their bright, unlined faces. The sky behind was always sky blue. Ozzie Sweet gave us heroes, and in Leifer's room in his family's apartment in the low-income housing project where he grew up on the Lower East Side of Manhattan, young Neil would tear out the Sweet photos of his beloved Brooklyn Dodger stars and tape them up on his walls.

So it was that when Leifer began to plan to troop the colors in 2005, he was thrilled to discover that Ozzie Sweet would be at Spring Training, too. The old photographer was 86, but still active, and so Leifer met with Sweet in Florida, and there he shot

OZZIE SWEET
NEW YORK YANKEES SPRING TRAINING CAMP,
TAMPA, FLORIDA
MARCH 2, 2005

Sweet shooting the Yankees of today—Jeter and Rodriquez and Matsui, yes, under a blue sky—just as he had posed DiMaggio and Berra and Mantle so many years ago when Neil was first learning how to work a camera, to focus and get the correct exposure, and then to compose and . . . click.

It was Ozzie Sweet's posed shots that first made Leifer aware of the beauty that the camera could capture. But Leifer soon began to see how sports photography could be so much more sophisticated. Among the photographs that first influenced him was one taken in 1960 at the Rome Olympics. The picture was taken by the late John Zimmerman—an uncommonly handsome, reflective man who was perhaps best known for advancing sports photography with many technical innovations that he conjured up. The Zimmerman shot that so impressed Leifer, however, was a simple enough one, of Abebe Bikila of Ethiopia, winning the Marathon.

Most all newspaper photographs of the time depicted Bikila full in the frame, making sure to show him from head to toe, inasmuch as he ran barefoot. In Zimmerman's great picture, though, the winner is but a small figure (his feet barely visible), as the photographer had chosen instead to portray the whole marvelous scene, there at the floodlit Arch of Constantine. Leifer had wished to own a camera with a long lens so that he could come in tight on the action, but in studying Zimmerman's masterwork, he understood how a sports photograph could show much more than the athlete, more even than the athlete victorious. Zimmerman had revealed the moment and the place and the man and the victory. He had, in a word, trapped history.

The picture was in black and white. The men in the crowd (and there are almost no women) were nearly all wearing coats and ties. It is utterly antique, more charm than drama. I talked to

SPORTS ILLUSTRATED COVER
THE TOKYO OLYMPIC GAMES
OCTOBER 19, 1964

SYLVESTER STALLONE AKA
ROCKY BALBOA
MANDALAY BAY HOTEL, LAS VEGAS, NEVADA
DECEMBER 4, 2005

Zimmerman a few years before he died about that picture, that Olympics. "God," he said, in reverie, "it was just all so romantic."

Leifer was breaking into the big-time then. He would shoot his first Olympic Games four years later in Tokyo, beating out all the other *SI* photographers for the opening ceremony cover shot, which he somehow managed to take squatting in an aisle. His cover—of the torchbearer—was printed in fast color, a marvel at the time. Soon enough, though, the Olympics, like all sports, were live on television, in living color, in your face. Leifer remembers shooting a huge football lineman sitting on the bench, the steam coming off him. It was, he knew, a terrific picture. Then he felt someone next to him. He turned to see a mobile TV cameraman, focusing on the very same player. And the red light was on. Leifer instantly realized that his wonderfully original picture was already obsolete.

To remain competitive against television, then, the still sports photographers had to work even harder. Ironically, there were more and more of them, too, aswarm at major events. The equipment became more sophisticated. The right exposure? The focus? Now the cameras did that for you. Incredibly, with the new digital equipment, it was possible even to defeat shadows, to reveal the whites of ballplayers' eyes beneath the brims of their caps. Leifer was leery of the new technology at first, but he began to grow more comfortable with it. He could not deny its greater efficacy. So it was that, from about the middle of his senior citizen's tour, Leifer himself worked almost exclusively with digital cameras.

When he began his year's journey through sports at the Rose Bowl on New Year's Day, 2005, which he shot from a helicopter three thousand feet up, Leifer was almost carefree. What fun this would be! All these great competitions, the world over—and him not bound by the score of the game. Shoot whatever you want! Ironically, however, soon enough, Leifer grew concerned; be careful what you wish for. He began to realize that, freed as he was from *having* to shoot what mattered most in the game, he damn well *had* to shoot absolutely great pictures.

This realization put him back in his old stride, pressured, competitive, ready to outshoot everybody else. The point was brought home even more dramatically when he found that young sports photographers—many of them women now in what had been strictly a man's world—would seek him out, bring him his books to autograph, ask to pose for pictures with him, tell him how he was their idol, their inspiration. He had come full circle, for now Neil Leifer was his Ozzie Sweet, his Ralph Morse, his John Zimmerman.

He tried to think of fresh approaches, how to best put new wine in old bottles. The beautiful can't-miss sixteenth green at Augusta, the spires at Churchill Downs, a president throwing out the first ball again in Washington, college football cheerleaders, even—yes—Rocky Balboa aka Sylvester Stallone, himself now working his own oldster gig. By the time Leifer had to return from Europe, after shooting Wimbledon, the Tour de France, and the British Open, he fell into his seat on the plane at Heathrow and suddenly all he could think was: *This is too good.*

Yes, but also: *This year is going too fast.*

The Hambletonian next, then the World Series, then Texas–Oklahoma football. The year was drawing to a close. Leifer began to search for additional events to shoot. His grandson playing pee-wee football, sumo wrestling—sumo wrestling!—figure skating, another NFL game. He didn't want it to end. December was playing out, and here is what Neil Leifer was thinking: *Just one more, just one more, just one . . . .*

—FRANK DEFORD

JANUARY

IF YOU'RE A REAL SPORTS FAN, you know months in advance what you'll be doing on certain days of the year. Photographers are no different. When I worked for *Sports Illustrated* my New Year's Day routine was set. I'd wake up in a hotel in Los Angeles, Miami, New Orleans, or Dallas. I'd grab a bite to eat. Then I'd go shoot the Rose, the Orange, the Sugar, or the Cotton Bowl. (Back then, all the big bowl games were on January 1.) Like a lot of people, I rang in the New Year with college football— I just did it on the road instead of in my den. I looked forward to it every year. CHOOSING THE FIRST STOP on my Senior Citizen Tour of the sports calendar was a no-brainer. I knew I wanted to do a New Year's Day game. As luck would have it, the Rose Bowl (Texas vs. Michigan) was the big one on January 1, 2005. I fell in love with the Rose Bowl stadium in 1960, when I saw an aerial shot of the game taken by one of my photography heroes, John Zimmerman. I'd always wanted to take a picture like that but never had the chance to. Whenever I covered a game I was looking for newsy shots—the winning touchdown, the key fumble. It's tough to get those if you're hovering in a helicopter. THIS WAS MY OPPORTUNITY. I figured getting great shots would be easy. I was very wrong. For one thing, in the post-9/11 world, you can't just charter a helicopter, fly over a stadium, and start snapping away. Security is unbelievably tight, and entering the airspace over the Bowl required difficult-to-get clearance. Even with the clearance, we were not permitted to fly lower than 3,000 feet. Ideally, I would have hovered at 800 feet. But I didn't give up, and I was able to get some beautiful shots (pages 32–35), pictures I'd wanted to shoot for many years. I knew my Tour was off to a great start. OF COURSE, championships are no longer won and lost on New Year's Day. So when the University of Southern California and Oklahoma played for the national title in the Orange Bowl three days later, I had to be there. (The Trojans won their second straight title.) I wanted to capture the pageantry of the game. So much of sports today is a corporate spectacle, and no shot illustrates that fact like one I took from the stands (pages 36–37). USC's Matt Leinart is handing off to Reggie Bush, who would win the Heisman Trophy later in the year, but it's hard to take your eyes off the giant FedEx logo on the field. JANUARY IS SYNONYMOUS WITH PRO FOOTBALL, too, and I've spent many a frigid day shooting NFL playoff games in places like Green Bay, Chicago, and Cleveland. Wintry conditions are a nightmare for photographers. Keeping lenses dry and trigger fingers warm is difficult. But cold and snow also always make for great football pictures, which is why I went to Philadelphia for the NFC Championship Game between the Eagles and the Falcons. A huge snowstorm was predicted; fortunately, it stopped snowing the morning of the game. But it was freezing, as you can tell from the throng of bundled-up photographers (pages 46–47). THAT'S A PICTURE that would have been impossible to get years ago. There probably weren't that many photographers—total—at championship games in the 1960s and '70s. But when the ball was inside the 10-yard-line they were stacked two-deep around the end zone in Philadelphia, everyone with state-of-the-art equipment. Talk about having to fight for your shot. When I started in this business, I never could have imagined that kind of scene.

THE ROSE BOWL
Texas vs. Michigan
Pasadena, California
January 1, 2005

TEXAS VS. MICHIGAN
The Rose Bowl
Pasadena, California
January 1, 2005

THE ORANGE BOWL

The National Championship Game
USC vs. Oklahoma
Miami, Florida
January 4, 2005

LEFT:
THE USC TROJANS

PAGES 40–41:
THE USC CHEERLEADERS
USC vs. Oklahoma, The Orange Bowl
Miami, Florida, January 4, 2005

JANUARY

NFC
CHAMPIONSHIP
GAME

EAGLES VS. FALCONS
PHILADELPHIA, PENNSYLVANIA
JANUARY 23, 2005

FALCONS QUARTERBACK
MICHAEL VICK

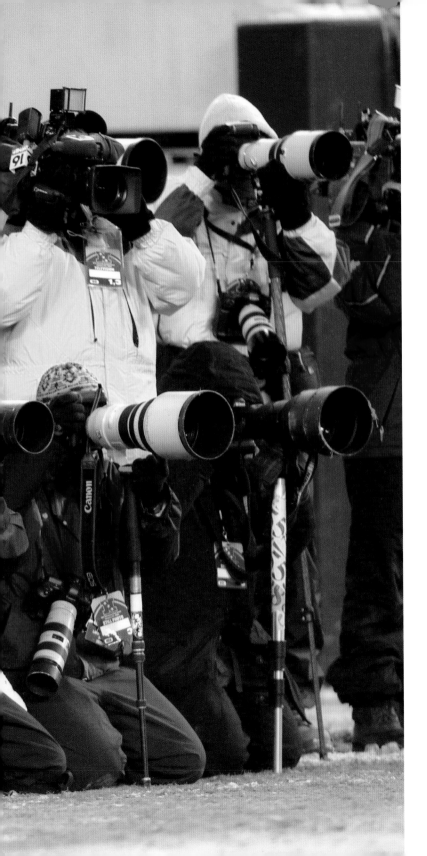

THE PHOTOGRAPHERS
Eagles vs. Falcons,
NFC Championship Game
Philadelphia, Pennsylvania
January 23, 2005

ABOVE:
CHARLIE CONNERLY (#42) AND
GINO MARCHETTI (#89)
GIANTS VS. COLTS, NFL CHAMPIONSHIP GAME
MEMORIAL STADIUM, BALTIMORE, MARYLAND
DECEMBER 27, 1959

OPPOSITE:
EAGLES QUARTERBACK
DONOVAN MCNABB
EAGLES VS. FALCONS,
NFC CHAMPIONSHIP GAME
PHILADELPHIA, PENNSYLVANIA
JANUARY 23, 2005

LEFT:
EAGLES QUARTERBACK
DONOVAN MCNABB

AND ABOVE
THE EAGLES AND FALCONS
TEAM MASCOTS
EAGLES VS. FALCONS,
NFC CHAMPIONSHIP GAME
PHILADELPHIA, PENNSYLVANIA
JANUARY 23, 2005

LEFT:
EAGLES TEAM OWNER
JEFFREY LURIE AT VICTORY
CELEBRATION
Eagles vs. Falcons,
NFC Championship Game
Philadelphia, Pennsylvania
January 23, 2005

OPPOSITE:
ALAN AMECHE AT
BALTIMORE COLTS VICTORY
CELEBRATION
Giants vs. Colts,
NFL Championship Game
Yankee Stadium, Bronx, New York
December 28, 1958

FEBRUARY

By the second month of the Senior Citizen Tour I was sure of one thing: I was smart to get out of the sports photography business when I did. It's not that I wasn't having fun. I even had a blast at the Daytona 500, where I forgot that auto racing has never been a favorite of mine. Before the Great American Race I traveled to Jacksonville, where the Patriots beat the Eagles in Super Bowl XXXIX. I saw something there that had caught my eye at the Orange Bowl: a television camera that hangs over the field, following the action on wires and pulleys. It practically puts viewers on the field. If you're a still photographer, how can you compete with that? Simply, you can't. I WAS DETERMINED to include that aerial camera in my Super Bowl shots. It wouldn't be the subject, but you couldn't help notice that it was there. The best one I took is of the Patriots defense waiting at the line of scrimmage while that camera peeks in on the Eagles' huddle (page 68). I wonder what those defenders would have given to be a fly on that camera lens. THE CAMERAS AREN'T ALL THAT'S CHANGED. The Super Bowl is bigger, louder, more crowded, and much more commercial. I thought the best way to document that growth was to duplicate a picture I took at the first Super Bowl, at the Los Angeles Coliseum in 1967. It's the pregame coin toss, with the two captains of each team and the referee at midfield (page 64). That's it, a grand total of five people surrounded by emerald green turf. A simple moment before what, in retrospect, was a very simple game. I DIDN'T THINK MUCH ABOUT THE PICTURE AT THE TIME, but it means much more when compared to the Super Bowl XXXIX coin toss (page 65). You see the Patriots' and

Eagles' captains. The officiating team. Camera crews. Kids from the Punt, Pass, and Kick program—even the Eagles mascot. There must be 70 people crammed into an area that held five at the first Super Bowl. During the national anthem two former Presidents, George H. W. Bush and Bill Clinton, were on hand. (All that was just the warm-up for the halftime show, which featured Paul McCartney and a fantastic fireworks display.) In 1967, the game was just that—a game. In 2005, it was a production, with some football sprinkled in the spectacle. I ORIGINALLY THOUGHT THE INDIANAPOLIS 500 was the obligatory race to visit on my tour. "Forget Indy," Steve Fine, *Sports Illustrated*'s director of photography, told me. "Daytona is the race you have to shoot." I knew what he meant as soon as I got to the track. The Daytona 500 is the Super Bowl of NASCAR, and it's hard to imagine a more perfect setting for a race. The crowds, the steeply banked turns, the deep blue sky—it's impossible not to take great pictures there. MY FAVORITE IS A SHOT OF THE RACE'S START (pages 72–73). To get it, I asked if I could shoot from the starter's stand, which really only had room for three people: the starter, the assistant starter, and the honorary starter, which was the actor Ashton Kutcher. (I had to elbow Ashton out of the way to get the shot.) It's one of the best auto racing pictures I've ever taken—and it was possible only because I was allowed in a spot most photographers never get permission to be in. I was starting to sense that I wasn't the only one excited about the Senior Citizen Tour. Everywhere I went people were treating me with respect and granting requests they'd usually refuse. It was as though they were happy to see me back in action. And I was thrilled to be there.

SUPER BOWL XXXIX

Eagles vs. Patriots
Jacksonville, Florida
February 6, 2005

PAUL MCCARTNEY AT HALFTIME

FEBRUARY

FLORIDA A&M MARCHING BAND
(PRE-GAME)
Eagles vs. Patriots, Super Bowl XXXIX
Jacksonville, Florida, February 6, 2005

PRESIDENTS BILL CLINTON
AND GEORGE H.W. BUSH DURING
THE NATIONAL ANTHEM
EAGLES VS. PATRIOTS, SUPER BOWL XXXIX
JACKSONVILLE, FLORIDA, FEBRUARY 6, 2005

FEBRUARY

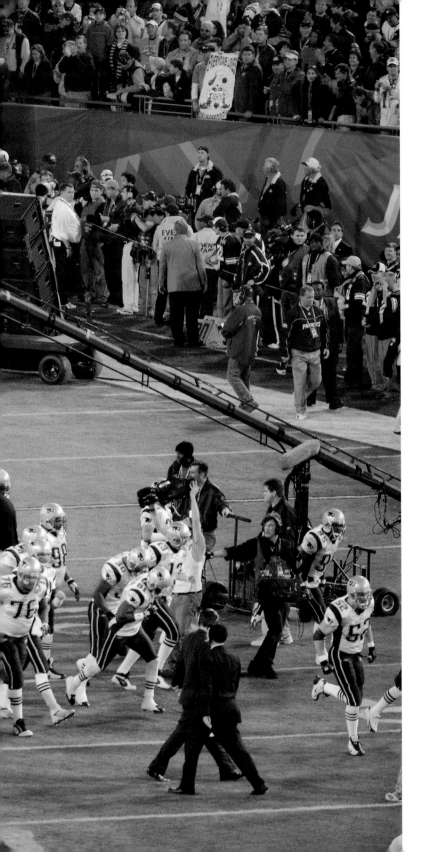

THE NEW ENGLAND PATRIOTS
EAGLES VS. PATRIOTS, SUPER BOWL XXXIX
JACKSONVILLE, FLORIDA, FEBRUARY 6, 2005

ABOVE:
COIN TOSS, GREEN BAY PACKERS
VS. KANSAS CITY CHIEFS
SUPER BOWL I
LOS ANGELES COLISEUM, JANUARY 15, 1967

OPPOSITE:
COIN TOSS, NEW ENGLAND PATRIOTS
VS. PHILADELPHIA EAGLES
SUPER BOWL XXXIX
JACKSONVILLE, FLORIDA, FEBRUARY 6, 2005

FEBRUARY

PAUL MCCARTNEY AT HALFTIME
Eagles vs. Patriots, Super Bowl XXXIX
Jacksonville, Florida, February 6, 2005

EAGLES HUDDLE AND
PATRIOTS DEFENSE
EAGLES VS. PATRIOTS, SUPER BOWL XXXIX
JACKSONVILLE, FLORIDA, FEBRUARY 6, 2005

QUARTERBACK TOM BRADY
AND THE PATRIOTS OFFENSE
Eagles vs. Patriots, Super Bowl XXXIX
Jacksonville, Florida, February 6, 2005

OPPOSITE:
PATRIOTS
QUARTERBACK
TOM BRADY

AND RIGHT:
POST GAME—THE
PATRIOTS ROMAN
PHIFER CELEBRATES
EAGLES VS. PATRIOTS,
SUPER BOWL XXXIX
JACKSONVILLE, FLORIDA
FEBRUARY 6, 2005

THE DAYTONA 500

DAYTONA INTERNATIONAL
SPEEDWAY
DAYTONA, FLORIDA
FEBRUARY 20, 2005

LEFT:
THE START OF THE DAYTONA 500

PAGES 74–75
THE MAIN STRAIGHTAWAY
AND GRANDSTAND

FEBRUARY

BETWEEN TURN 3 AND TURN 4
The Daytona 500
Daytona International Speedway
Daytona, Florida, February 20, 2005

FEBRUARY

MARCH

ONE OF THE GREAT THINGS about spring training is that every day is Old Timers' Day. Teams invite their great players from years past to camp, and it's not unusual to see Sandy Koufax tutoring a Dodgers pitcher in Vero Beach or Reggie Jackson holding court with Yankees sluggers in Tampa. They have titles like "roving instructor" and "special assistant," but mostly the Hall of Famers are there to tell stories and wave to the crowd. If you're a fan—or a photographer—my age, it's heaven. It's wonderful to see your heroes walk out of the history books, in uniform, and come to life every spring. I WAS REMINDED OF THIS when my tour took me to Yankees camp. Where else are you going to get a picture of Yogi Berra sitting next to Graig Nettles and Frank Howard, a 1964 *Sports Illustrated* cover subject of mine (page 88)? Now, as a kid I was a Brooklyn Dodgers fan, and I hated the Yankees. But I made an exception for one of their stars. It was impossible to dislike Yogi. I also love him as a subject, and one look at the portrait I shot in the dugout (page 89) makes it easy to understand why. BUT I DIDN'T TRAVEL TO TAMPA to shoot Yogi. I was there to see another favorite from my youth: Ozzie Sweet, the longtime photographer for *Sport* magazine. Ozzie used to take beautiful posed, color pictures of all the great athletes in the 1950s and '60s, and many of his Dodger pictures were Scotch-taped to my bedroom wall. Before spring training I heard that Ozzie, at age 86, would be shooting the Yankees. I had never met him and was fascinated by the idea of watching him work, so I called him up. He agreed to let me photograph him at work. Ozzie, who's a great storyteller and still sharp as a tack, had the Yankees eating out of his hand. Joe Torre, Derek Jeter, Alex Rodriguez, Randy Johnson, Hideki Matsui—Ozzie posed them against a dazzlingly blue sky, and I took in the entire scene. It was terrific to watch Ozzie in action. The danger of meeting legends like him is that so often they don't measure up to what you wanted them to be. That definitely wasn't the case with Ozzie, and I'm thrilled to now be his friend as well as his fan. I was never the kind of photographer who became friends with the athletes I shot. It's not that we didn't get along; it's just that my relationships were purely professional. The exception is Muhammad Ali. When I met him in the mid-1960s it never entered my mind that I'd be shooting him four decades later, or that he would become a dear friend. I thought it would be a nice addition to the Tour if Ali and I recreated a picture that was taken of us almost 40 years earlier. We met at the Omni Shoreham Hotel in Washington, D.C., on St. Patrick's Day, and I was pleased to see Muhammad looking so good. He has Parkinson's disease and some days are better than others, but on this day he looked like the Ali of old. I think these pictures are the perfect way to document our long relationship. I'll never forget the time, about two years ago, that I asked Muhammad to sign a print of that 1966 picture of us. He took a long look at it, smiled, and said, "Nothing's changed. I'm still prettier than you are."

SPRING TRAINING
New York Yankees
Training Camp
Tampa, Florida
March 2, 2005

ALEX RODRIGUEZ AND
OZZIE SWEET

PAGES 82–83:
DEREK JETER, JOE TORRE, AND
OZZIE SWEET

RANDY JOHNSON AND OZZIE SWEET
New York Yankees Spring Training Camp
Tampa, Florida, March 2, 2005

MARCH

OZZIE SWEET AND HIDEKI MATSUI
New York Yankees Spring Training Camp
Tampa, Florida, March 2, 2005

ABOVE:
GUEST COACHES FRANK HOWARD,
GRAIG NETTLES, AND YOGI BERRA

AND OPPOSITE:
YOGI BERRA
NEW YORK YANKEES SPRING TRAINING CAMP
TAMPA, FLORIDA, MARCH 2, 2005

MARCH

MUHAMMAD ALI AND NEIL LEIFER

LEFT:
MUHAMMAD ALI AND
NEIL LEIFER
SPORTS ILLUSTRATED STUDIO,
NEW YORK, NEW YORK
DECEMBER 1966

OPPOSITE:
MUHAMMAD ALI AND
NEIL LEIFER
OMNI SHOREHAM HOTEL,
WASHINGTON, D.C.
MARCH 17, 2005

APRIL THE KEY TO A SPECTACULAR SHOT is often being in the right place at the right time. But that doesn't mean it's always luck. Sometimes you stake out a can't-miss position. Sometimes you lobby for access others don't have. And sometimes you look for a unique angle. I did all three in April. I WANTED TO SHOOT THE FINAL FOUR in St. Louis from above, where I'd be able to incorporate the Final Four logo as a recurring element in most of my shots. So instead of setting up shop on the baseline as I usually would, I took all of my pictures from the catwalk directly over the court at the Edward Jones Dome. It was more than worth it, especially in the championship game. Every moment made for good pictures, from the handshake before the opening tap (page 102) to the victorious North Carolina Tar Heels posing with their trophy (pages 104–05). I TOOK A MORE CONVENTIONAL APPROACH at the Masters the following weekend. My favorite hole at Augusta has always been the par-3 No. 16. It's breathtakingly beautiful, and in the late afternoon the huge crowd and the blooming azaleas are reflected in the lake that runs from tee to green. I shot 16 as much as I could during the tournament, and on Sunday it really paid off. I got exactly the shot I was after: Tiger Woods striding across the green with the late-afternoon sunlight—photographers call it "magic hour"—glinting off his club (pages 114–15). As a bonus, I found myself in perfect position for one of the magical moments in Masters history. On 16 Woods, who won his fourth green jacket, sank an incredible birdie chip, one of the greatest golf shots ever. My picture of Tiger and his caddie celebrating (page 116) mirrors my *SI* cover of Jack Nicklaus in the same spot in 1972 (page 117).

I finished April at the Penn Relays at Philadelphia's Franklin Field, one of my favorite old stadiums. But by far the highlight of my year was when President George W. Bush threw out the first pitch at the Washington Nationals' home opener. I wanted a behind-the-scenes look at what it's like when the president of the United States goes to a baseball game, and months before I sent a letter to Andy Card, the then White House chief of staff. I suggested it would be fascinating to shadow the president on his visit to RFK Stadium, and I was pleasantly surprised when I heard that Bush himself had approved my request. I was really inside the inner circle that night. The Secret Service detail was behind me, and I spent most of the evening within ten feet of the president. It was exhilarating. I rode in the presidential motorcade (the trip from the White House to RFK took eight minutes) and photographed President Bush as he threw a strike in front of 44,000 people. Before the game I shot him as he warmed up in an indoor batting cage and as he chatted up players in the clubhouse. (The official White House photographer and I were the only ones taking pictures in the cage and, later, in the president's private box.) Bush really is a friendly guy, and he puts everyone at ease. You could tell how much the president enjoyed himself. Just before the game began I asked the president if I could take a portrait of him and the First Lady (pages 126–27). They happily obliged and smiled broadly, just a couple of fans taking in a ballgame. As for me, I ended up with a great set of pictures—including one of the president and me—and a baseball he autographed for me. It was an evening I'll never forget.

THE FINAL FOUR
EDWARD JONES DOME,
ST. LOUIS, MISSOURI
APRIL 2 & 4, 2005

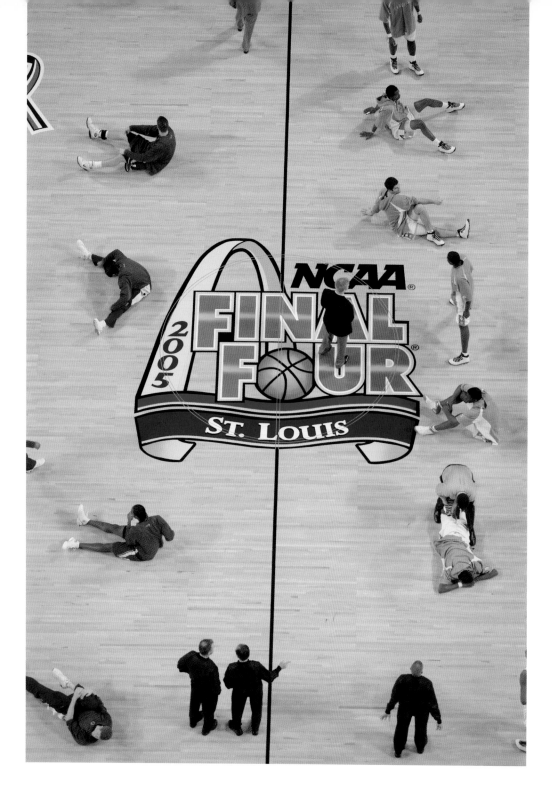

LEFT:
PRE-GAME WARM UP
MICHIGAN VS.
NORTH CAROLINA
THE FINAL FOUR—SEMIFINAL
EDWARD JONES DOME,
ST. LOUIS, MISSOURI
APRIL 2, 2005

OPPOSITE:
THE OPENING TAP OF
THE CHAMPIONSHIP
GAME
JAWAD WILLIAMS (#21) AND
JAMES AUGUSTINE (#40)
ILLINOIS VS. NORTH
CAROLINA
THE FINAL FOUR
EDWARD JONES DOME,
ST. LOUIS, MISSOURI
APRIL 4, 2005

PAGES 98–99:
ILLINOIS VS.
LOUISVILLE
THE FINAL FOUR—SEMIFINAL
EDWARD JONES DOME,
ST. LOUIS, MISSOURI
APRIL 2, 2005

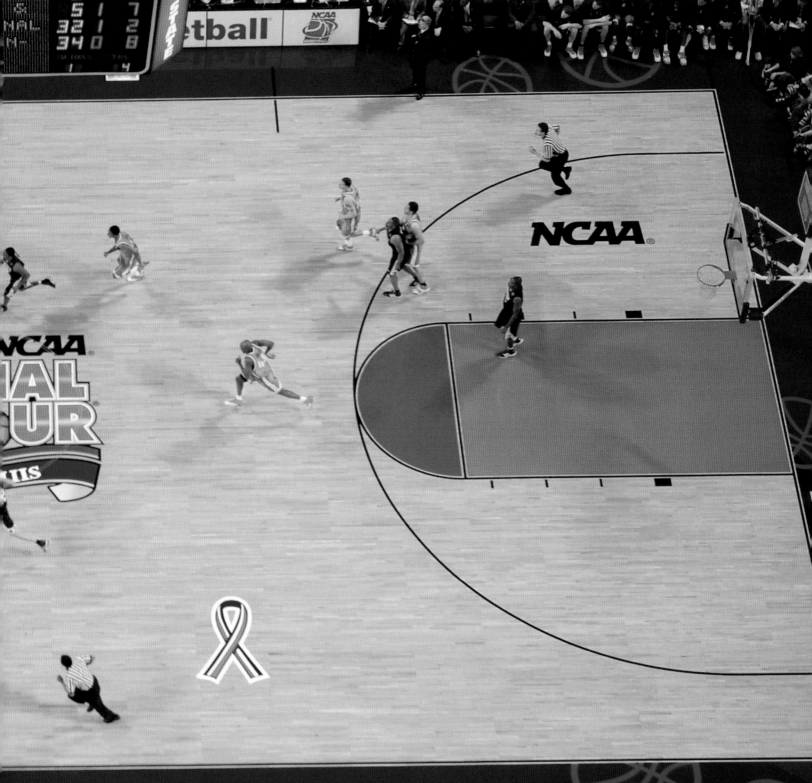

ABOVE:
TIME-OUT—COACH ROY WILLIAMS
AND THE NORTH CAROLINA
TAR HEELS
Illinois vs. North Carolina, The Final Four
Edward Jones Dome, St. Louis, Missouri
April 4, 2005

OPPOSITE:
THE TAR HEELS' SEAN MAY (#42)
Illinois vs. North Carolina,
Championship Game, The Final Four
Edward Jones Dome, St. Louis, Missouri
April 4, 2005

APRIL

SEAN MAY (#42) AND
LUTHER HEAD (#4)
ILLINOIS VS. NORTH CAROLINA
CHAMPIONSHIP GAME, THE FINAL FOUR
EDWARD JONES DOME, ST. LOUIS, MISSOURI
APRIL 4, 2005

THE TAR HEELS CELEBRATE THEIR
VICTORY
Illinois vs. North Carolina,
Championship Game, The Final Four
Edward Jones Dome, St. Louis, Missouri
April 4, 2005

THE NATIONAL CHAMPIONS—
THE NORTH CAROLINA TAR HEELS
The Final Four
Edward Jones Dome, St. Louis, Missouri
April 4, 2005

APRIL

THE MASTERS
THE AUGUSTA NATIONAL GOLF COURSE, AUGUSTA, GEORGIA
APRIL 7–10, 2005

LEFT:
TIGER WOODS TEEING OFF
ON THE 4TH HOLE

PAGES 108–09:
THE AZALEAS BEHIND THE
16TH GREEN

APRIL

APRIL

TIGER WOODS ON THE 16TH GREEN
The Masters
The Augusta National Golf Course,
Augusta, Georgia, April 9, 2005

JACK NICKLAUS ON THE 16TH GREEN
The Masters
The Augusta National Golf Course,
Augusta, Georgia, April 1975

APRIL

OPPOSITE:
TIGER WOODS CELEBRATING
ON THE 16TH HOLE
The Masters
The Augusta National Golf Course,
Augusta, Georgia, April 10, 2005

RIGHT:
JACK NICKLAUS CELEBRATING
ON THE 16TH HOLE
The Masters
The Augusta National Golf Course,
Augusta, Georgia, April 17, 1972

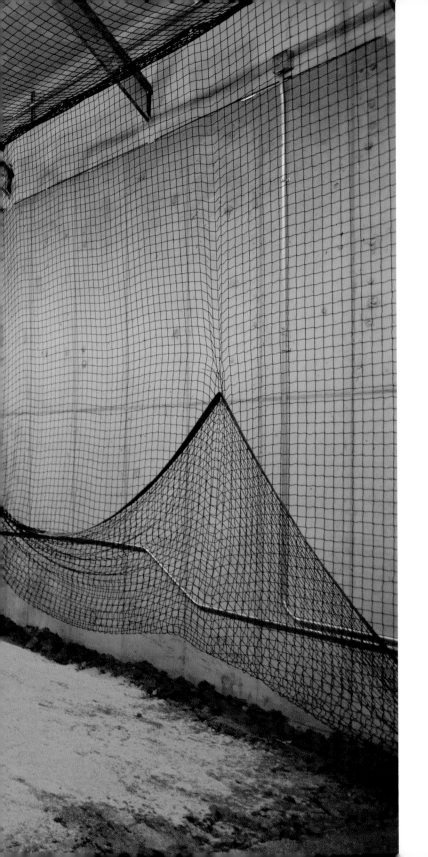

OPENING DAY
The Washington Nationals
RFK Stadium
Washington, D.C.
April 14, 2005

PRESIDENT GEORGE W. BUSH
WARMING UP

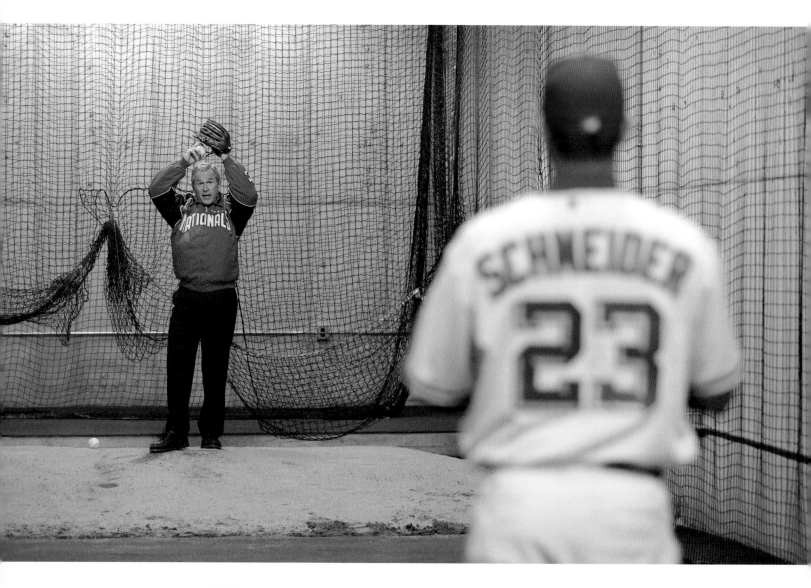

ABOVE:
PRESIDENT BUSH WARMING UP
WITH WASHINGTON NATIONALS
CATCHER BRIAN SCHNEIDER

AND OPPOSITE:
PRESIDENT BUSH WITH
WASHINGTON NATIONALS
CATCHER BRIAN SCHNEIDER
THE WASHINGTON NATIONALS
OPENING DAY—RFK STADIUM
WASHINGTON, D.C., APRIL 14, 2005

APRIL

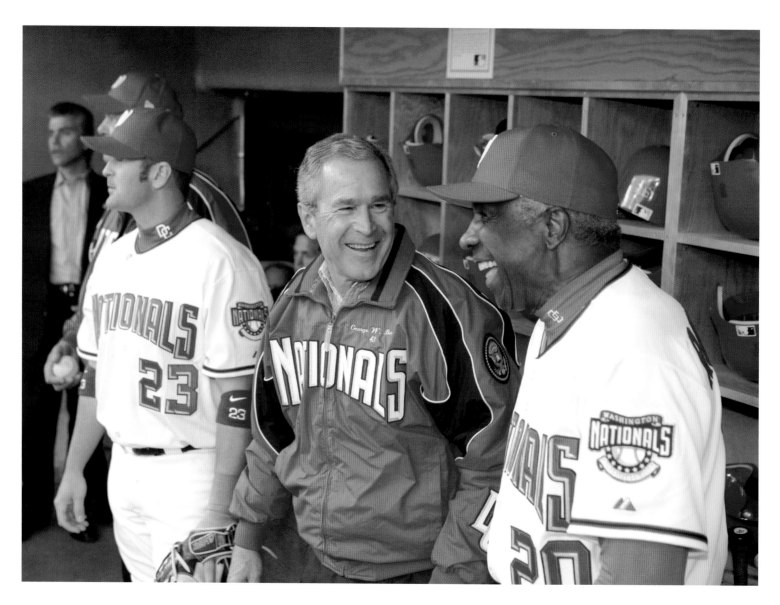

ABOVE:
PRESIDENT BUSH AND
WASHINGTON NATIONALS'
MANAGER FRANK ROBINSON

AND OPPOSITE:
PRESIDENT BUSH THROWS OUT
CEREMONIAL FIRST PITCH
The Washington Nationals
Opening Day—RFK Stadium
Washington, D.C., April 14, 2005

BELOW:
**PRESIDENT JOHN F. KENNEDY
AND VICE-PRESIDENT
LYNDON JOHNSON**
Opening Day—Griffith Stadium,
Washington, D.C., April 10, 1961

OPPOSITE:
PRESIDENT GEORGE W. BUSH
The Washington Nationals
Opening Day—RFK Stadium
Washington, D.C., April 14, 2005

APRIL

PRESIDENT GEORGE W. BUSH AND
FIRST LADY LAURA BUSH
The Washington Nationals
Opening Day—RFK Stadium
Washington, D.C., April 14, 2005

THE PENN RELAYS
FRANKLIN FIELD,
PHILADELPHIA, PENNSYLVANIA
APRIL 29, 2005

THE PENN RELAYS
FRANKLIN FIELD, PHILADELPHIA, PENNSYLVANIA
APRIL 29, 2005

APRIL

THE 131ST
KENTUCKY DERBY

CHURCHILL DOWNS,
LOUISVILLE, KENTUCKY
MAY 7, 2005

PAGES 138–39:
THE 131ST KENTUCKY OAKS—
POST PARADE
THE 131ST KENTUCKY DERBY
CHURCHILL DOWNS, LOUISVILLE, KENTUCKY
MAY 6, 2005

MAY

OPPOSITE:
THE RUN FOR THE ROSES
THE 131ST KENTUCKY DERBY
CHURCHILL DOWNS, LOUISVILLE, KENTUCKY
MAY 7, 2005

BELOW:
THE START OF THE DERBY
THE 91ST KENTUCKY DERBY
CHURCHILL DOWNS, LOUISVILLE, KENTUCKY
MAY 1, 1965

GIACOMO (#10, LEFT)
WINS THE DERBY
THE 131ST KENTUCKY DERBY
CHURCHILL DOWNS, LOUISVILLE, KENTUCKY
MAY 7, 2005

BELOW:
GIACOMO IN THE WINNERS' CIRCLE
OWNERS MR. & MRS. JEROME S.
MOSS, JOCKEY MIKE SMITH
THE 131ST KENTUCKY DERBY
CHURCHILL DOWNS, LOUISVILLE, KENTUCKY
MAY 7, 2005

OPPOSITE:
LUCKY DEBONAIRE IN THE
WINNERS' CIRCLE
JOCKEY WILLIE SHOEMAKER
THE 91ST KENTUCKY DERBY
CHURCHILL DOWNS, LOUISVILLE, KENTUCKY
MAY 1, 1965

ABOVE:
THE 40TH ANNIVERSARY OF
ALI VS. LISTON
THE COLISEE (FORMERLY KNOWN AS
ST. DOMINIC'S ARENA)
LEWISTON, MAINE, MAY 25, 2005

OPPOSITE:
MUHAMMAD ALI VS. SONNY LISTON
ST. DOMINIC'S ARENA, LEWISTON, MAINE
MAY 25, 1965

MAY

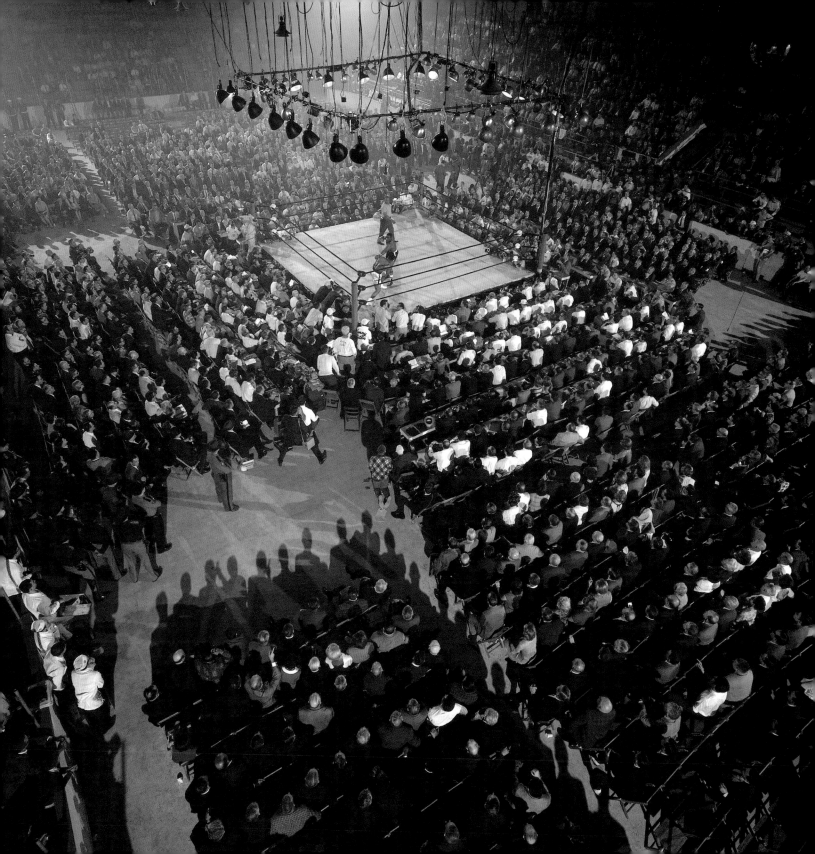

JUNE

WHEN I STARTED SHOOTING BASKETBALL in the 1960s, dominant big men ruled the game. In the NBA the kings were Bill Russell and Wilt Chamberlain. Then UCLA landed Lew Alcindor, before he was known as Kareem Abdul-Jabbar. Today, Shaquille O'Neal walks in their giant footsteps— though, at 7'1" and well over 300 pounds, Shaq would have had a significant size advantage over all three. SHAQ PLAYS A MUCH MORE PHYSICAL GAME than those big men did. I wanted to capture that power when his Miami Heat played the Detroit Pistons in the NBA's Eastern Conference Finals. Shaq couldn't lead the Heat to victory in the series. But as a subject he's a champion, whether he's posing for a portrait or playing the game. The brute force he brings to the court makes for great photographs. On defense, he's a man among boys. When he drives to the hoop, bodies go flying in every direction. It seemed like there were four Pistons leaning on Shaq at all times, bumping and hacking him throughout the game. After seeing that, no one can tell me that basketball isn't a contact sport. OF COURSE, no athlete has ever been more synonymous with pure power than Mike Tyson. Boxing is far and away my favorite sport to shoot—I've photographed just about every heavyweight champ since Floyd Patterson—and I had hoped to shoot a heavyweight title fight during the Senior Citizen Tour. Since there weren't any marquee bouts scheduled, I went to see Tyson take on a pug named Kevin McBride in Washington, D.C. WHEN IRON MIKE WAS IN HIS PRIME his opponents didn't simply go down. They crumbled. I saw it firsthand in 1986, when he knocked Trevor Berbick silly to become the youngest-ever heavyweight champion (page 162). I expected Tyson to show flashes of his youth against McBride. The fight was supposed to be a setup, an easy win to help him rebuild his career at age 38. IN HIS DRESSING ROOM BEFORE THE FIGHT, Tyson looked like he was in great shape. He was in a great mood, too. He joked around and posed for a picture with my son Corey, whom I had brought along. He looked strong in the early rounds, but then something happened. McBride landed a few punches, and Tyson lost the will to fight. He went down in the sixth round. It didn't look like McBride hit him that hard, but Tyson just sat there on the canvas, leaning against the ropes with a blank look in his eyes (page 165). When you look at that picture, it's hard to believe it's the same man who was once so ferocious in the ring. THERE WAS A PLEASANT SURPRISE IN WASHINGTON: The day before the Tyson bout I heard that Laila Ali, Muhammad's daughter, was fighting on the undercard. I'm not a big fan of women's boxing, but I was excited to photograph Laila in action. Plus, Muhammad himself made an unexpected appearance. Laila is beautiful and a great subject, just like her dad, and I really like the picture I got of Muhammad clowning with his daughter in her dressing room (pages 158–59). A FEW WEEKS LATER I flew to England for Wimbledon, where on the final day of June I saw the women's semifinal between Maria Sharapova and Venus Williams. I was there to shoot Sharapova—she was the defending Wimbledon champion and is one of the most stunning subjects in sports. But I became quite taken with Venus, whom I had never photographed before. She emotes in ways that you just can't fake and is every bit as charismatic as Shaq. Sharapova had drawn me to Wimbledon, but I found it hard to root against Venus. One court, two great subjects—it was a win-win situation for a photographer.

NBA PLAYOFFS
Miami Heat vs.
Detroit Pistons
Miami, Florida
June 2, 2005

THE HEAT'S SHAQUILLE O'NEAL

THE HEAT'S SHAQUILLE O'NEAL
Miami Heat vs. Detroit Pistons
NBA Playoffs
Miami, Florida, June 2, 2005

JUNE

LEFT:
WILT CHAMBERLAIN
AND BILL RUSSELL
PHILADELPHIA WARRIORS VS.
BOSTON CELTICS
NBA PLAYOFFS
PHILADELPHIA, PENNSYLVANIA
APRIL 11, 1967

OPPOSITE:
THE HEAT'S
SHAQUILLE O'NEAL
MIAMI HEAT VS. DETROIT PISTONS
NBA PLAYOFFS
MIAMI, FLORIDA
JUNE 2, 2005

DETROIT'S LINDSEY HUNTER (#10)
AND MIAMI'S SHAQUILLE O'NEAL
Miami Heat vs. Detroit Pistons
NBA Playoffs
Miami, Florida, June 2, 2005

157

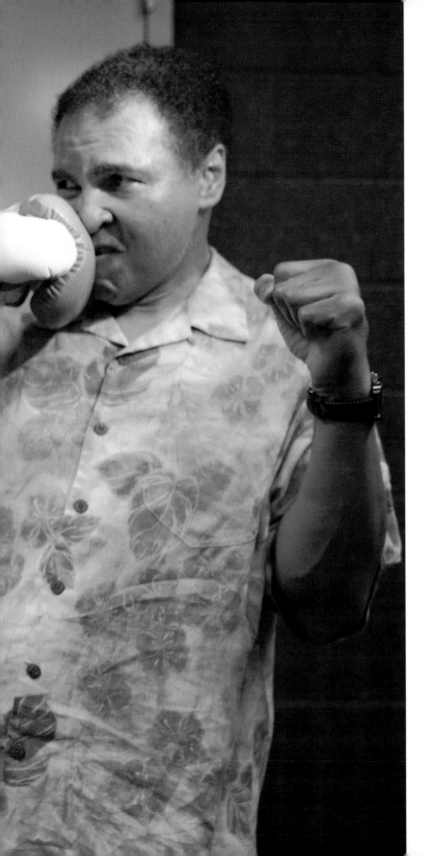

MIKE TYSON VS. KEVIN MCBRIDE

LAILA ALI VS. ERIN TOUGHILL
Washington, D.C.
June 11, 2005

PREFIGHT: MUHAMMAD ALI WITH
DAUGHTER LAILA ALI

PAGE 160:
LAILA ALI
Laila Ali vs. Erin Toughill
Washington, D.C., June 11, 2005

PAGE 161:
MIKE TYSON
Mike Tyson vs. Kevin McBride
Washington, D.C., June 11, 2005

JUNE

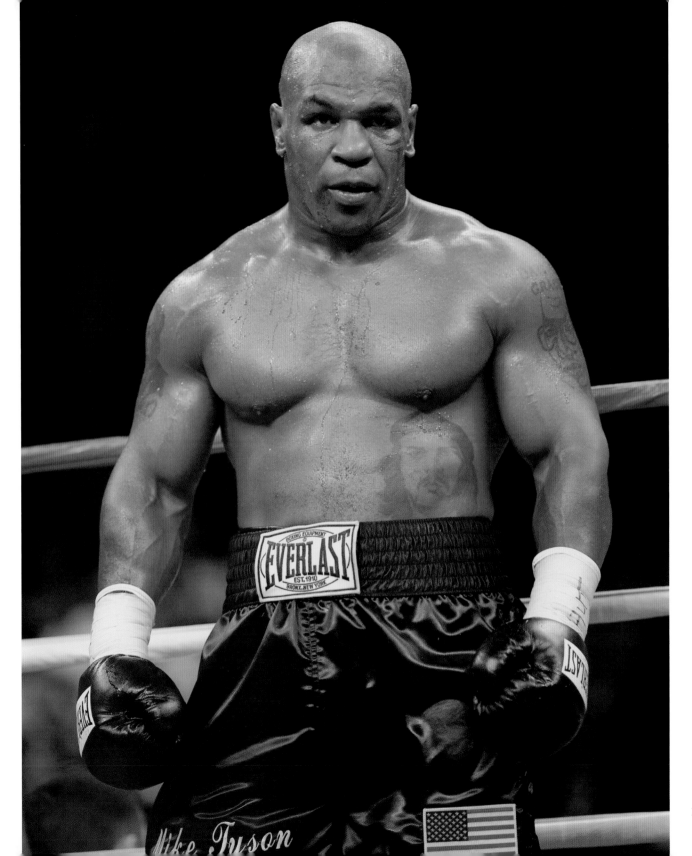

ABOVE:
TYSON BECOMES HEAVYWEIGHT
CHAMPION
Mike Tyson vs. Trevor Berbick
Heavyweight title fight
Las Vegas, Nevada, November 22, 1986

OPPOSITE:
MIKE TYSON VS. KEVIN MCBRIDE
Washington, D.C., June 11, 2005

JUNE

ABOVE AND OPPOSITE:
MIKE TYSON VS. KEVIN MCBRIDE
Washington, D.C.
June 11, 2005

PAGES 166–167
LAILA ALI VS. ERIN TOUGHILL

MUHAMMAD ALI WITH DAUGHTER
LAILA AND BROTHER RAHAMAN
Laila Ali vs. Erin Toughill
Washington, D.C., June 11, 2005

JUNE

WIMBLEDON
Venus Williams vs.
Maria Sharapova
Ladies' Singles Semifinal
The All England Club,
Wimbledon, England
June 30, 2005

VENUS WILLIAMS VS.
MARIA SHARAPOVA
LADIES' SINGLES SEMIFINAL, WIMBLEDON
THE ALL ENGLAND CLUB, WIMBLEDON, ENGLAND
JUNE 30, 2005

BJORN BORG VS. ILIE NASTASE
GENTLEMEN'S SINGLES FINAL, WIMBLEDON
THE ALL ENGLAND CLUB, WIMBLEDON, ENGLAND
JULY 3, 1976

VENUS WILLIAMS WINS THE
LADIES' SINGLES SEMIFINAL
Venus Williams vs. Maria Sharapova
Wimbledon
The All England Club, Wimbledon, England
June 30, 2005

JUNE

JULY

THERE ARE TWO KINDS OF CHAMPIONS, and at Wimbledon each had a moment in the sun. (And sometimes the clouds—it was England, after all.) Venus Williams is a godsend for photographers. She complements her athleticism with unbridled enthusiasm and emotion; every time you look at her there's a great picture. Venus was a long shot at Wimbledon, and she clearly enjoyed her unlikely run. I love the contrast between her excitement and the stiff-upper-lip Wimbledon backdrop. ROGER FEDERER, THE MEN'S CHAMPION, is at the opposite end of the charisma spectrum. He's an incredible player, but he's a robot. He barely sweats. His face is expressionless. When he hoists his trophy, it's hard to tell if he won, lost, or just finished doing his taxes. In fact, my favorite shot of him is one where he has his back to the camera (page 185). The fans look happier than he does, and it's a wonderful 21st-century Wimbledon moment. Nearly everyone is preserving the scene with a digital camera or cell phone. WIMBLEDON WAS THE FIRST STOP on the Senior Citizen Tour's European swing. Next was the Tour de France, though I only had time for two days there, because I wanted to see Jack Nicklaus play his final British Open. I opted for a good photo of Lance Armstrong in the mountain stages in the Alps, where he always excels, and on my second day, on a beautiful turn on the Col du Galibier, I hit the jackpot. I set up a remote camera with a wide-angle lens and got a great shot of Lance, wearing the leader's yellow jersey, and the pack with the snow-capped Alps rising in the background. With my handheld camera I photographed Lance being escorted by his Discovery teammates up a climb (pages 186–87). They were his protection, ensuring that no one got in his way as he rode to his seventh Tour de France victory. The picture tells a great story about the world's premier bicycle event. Now my mission was to get to the British Open. As at the Masters, Tiger Woods was the show, and I got some great shots of him conquering the fabled Old Course at St. Andrews. But for sure, Nicklaus and the course itself were the co-stars of the tournament. St. Andrews is one of golf's cathedrals, and Jack was always one of my favorite subjects. Even though he didn't make the cut, watching him play his final British Open rounds was one of the most emotional moments of my year. I'm particularly fond of my shot of Jack standing with his son Steve, his caddie for the Open (page 196). It had to be a great thrill for Jack and his son to walk the Old Course together. I know, because I had a similar experience. My son, Corey, was with me, working as my photo assistant. Corey is a huge sports fan and an avid golfer, but even when he was a kid we never went to many events together. When I left *Sports Illustrated* in 1978, he was seven years old, so he was too young to come with me when I was covering Super Bowls and World Series every year. When he was older, I was too busy with other assignments to take in many sporting events. Corey is 35 now, a successful attorney, but one of the things that made the Senior Citizen Tour special was that it gave us a chance to bond in a way we hadn't before. Together we saw the Orange Bowl, Super Bowl, Daytona 500, Kentucky Derby, Masters, an NBA playoff game, the British Open, a Mike Tyson fight, the Texas–Oklahoma game, and a Dallas Cowboys game—a dream year for any sports fan. The major sports events have been such a huge part of my life, and now those experiences are part of Corey's too. I'm glad, after all these years, I was able to share them with him.

WIMBLEDON
Ladies' Singles Final—
Venus Williams vs.
Lindsey Davenport

Gentlemen's Singles Final—
Roger Federer vs.
Andy Roddick
The All England Club,
Wimbledon, England
July 2–3, 2005

LEFT THROUGH PAGE 179:
VENUS WILLIAMS

JULY

TOUR DE FRANCE
On the Col du Galibier
11th stage, Courchevel
to Briançon, France
July 13, 2005

LANCE ARMSTRONG (YELLOW JERSEY)

ON THE COL DU GALIBIER
11TH STAGE, COURCHEVEL TO BRIANÇON, FRANCE
TOUR DE FRANCE
JULY 13, 2005

LANCE ARMSTRONG (YELLOW JERSEY)
On the Col du Galibier
11th stage, Courchevel to Briançon, France
Tour de France
July 13, 2005

A LONE CYCLIST ON THE
COL DU GALIBIER
11TH STAGE, COURCHEVEL TO BRIANÇON, FRANCE
TOUR DE FRANCE
JULY 13, 2005

THE BRITISH OPEN
THE OLD COURSE, ST. ANDREWS, SCOTLAND
JULY 15–17, 2005

TIGER WOODS ON THE 18TH TEE

PAGE 196:
JACK NICKLAUS AND HIS CADDIE,
SON STEVE, ON THE 17TH GREEN

PAGE 197:
JACK NICKLAUS ON THE 17TH GREEN

RIGHT:
JACK NICKLAUS WAVES FAREWELL
FROM THE SWILCAN BRIDGE ON
THE 18TH HOLE
The Old Course, The British Open
St. Andrews, Scotland, July 15, 2005

TIGER WOODS
The Old Course, The British Open
St. Andrews, Scotland, July 17, 2005

TIGER WOODS
The Old Course, The British Open
St. Andrews, Scotland, July 17, 2005

ABOVE:
THE FINAL LEADERBOARD

AND OPPOSITE:
THE 2005 BRITISH OPEN
CHAMPION, TIGER WOODS
The Old Course, The British Open
St. Andrews, Scotland, July 17, 2005

AUGUST

I STARTED MY SENIOR CITIZEN TOUR taking pictures the way I always had, on film. That's what I was comfortable with, though almost all of today's sports shooters use nothing but digital photography. I'll bet some of the younger ones don't even know what a roll of film looks like. Well, gradually I saw the light. At first I only shot digital for night and indoor events like the Super Bowl and the Final Four and continued to use film for daytime events like the Masters, the Kentucky Derby, and the Daytona 500. I eventually discovered what all the fuss was about. Digital is far superior, and carrying a handful of memory cards sure beats lugging hundreds of rolls of film through the airport. If I did it all over again, I'd have used digital for the entire year. ONE OF THE BEST THINGS ABOUT DIGITAL PHOTOGRAPHY is that it provides instant gratification. You shoot, then you check the back of the camera to see what you have. By the time I went to Europe at the end of June I was shooting digital exclusively, and as I flew home from the British Open, I already knew my swing through Wimbledon, the Tour de France, and St. Andrews had been a big success. It was a nice feeling, especially since I was heading into what was always a relaxing time of year when I was with *Sports Illustrated*. August is a slow month on the sports calendar. Baseball's pennant races aren't quite in gear. Football season is still a few weeks away. August was a chance for me to take it easy and recharge for the busy autumn ahead. THERE WAS ONE EVENT THAT I WANTED TO COVER IN AUGUST—the Hambletonian, which was once considered the Kentucky Derby of harness racing. When I was a young photographer in the early 1960s harness racing was still very popular. Every sports fan knew what the Hambletonian was. More important to me, harness racing always lent itself to great photographs. So mid-month I headed to Meadowlands Racetrack in New Jersey, where the Hambletonian is now run. THESE DAYS THE RACE IS HARDLY A MARQUEE EVENT. Few sports fans have even heard of it. The track at the Du Quoin, Illinois, state fairgrounds, where the race was run for many years, was low-key and quaint, a place where trotting fans wandered over from the adjacent state fair, and the racecourse was lined with trees and little else (page 213). I enjoyed going there because it was so different from Yankee Stadium and the Orange Bowl and the other stadiums I usually worked in. It looks positively prehistoric compared to the Meadowlands, which has a 40,000-seat grandstand, glassed-in luxury boxes, and gourmet restaurants overlooking the track and the Manhattan skyline rising behind the first turn. THE MEADOWLANDS TRACK IS BEAUTIFUL, especially on a bright late-summer day, but I realized some things hadn't changed about the Hambletonian. Harness racing still makes for great photos. And even if it's not as popular as it once was, harness racing still has a unique beauty and grace. Shooting the Hambletonian was a nice break from the front-page events that I had been experiencing on the Tour. This was more intimate, a place where people gathered simply because they enjoy harness racing. With all the hype and gloss that surround our games now, it's easy to forget that love of a sport is what made us fans in the first place.

THE HAMBLETONIAN
THE MEADOWLANDS,
NEW JERSEY
AUGUST 6, 2005

VIVID PHOTO AND DRIVER ROGER
HAMMER DURING THE PRERACE

AUGUST

OPPOSITE:

THE START OF THE 2005
HAMBLETONIAN
THE HAMBLETONIAN
THE MEADOWLANDS, NEW JERSEY
AUGUST 6, 2005

BELOW:

THE START OF THE 1961
HAMBLETONIAN
THE HAMBLETONIAN
THE ILLINOIS STATE FAIRGROUNDS,
DU QUOIN, ILLINOIS, AUGUST 30, 1961

AUGUST

THE TURN FOR HOME AT
THE MEADOWLANDS
THE HAMBLETONIAN
THE MEADOWLANDS, NEW JERSEY
AUGUST 6, 2005

THE BACKSTRETCH AT THE
ILLINOIS STATE FAIRGROUNDS
THE HAMBLETONIAN
THE ILLINOIS STATE FAIRGROUNDS,
DU QUOIN, ILLINOIS, AUGUST 30, 1961

SEPTEMBER

MARIA SHARAPOVA is as dazzling a subject as a sports photographer will ever find. I don't remember another world-class athlete who could have made it into *Sports Illustrated's* Swimsuit Issue, as Sharapova did in 2006, based solely on her own beauty. I was very excited to get another chance to shoot Sharapova at the U.S. Open, which she entered as the No. 1 seed. The Open lends itself to great photos—especially in late afternoon, when courts are bathed in the fading New York sunlight. There's a reason it's called "magic hour." In that setting, with a subject like Sharapova—who, in addition to being drop-dead beautiful, is every bit as charismatic as Venus Williams—good shots are hard to miss. I LUCKED OUT WITH THE MEN'S DRAW, TOO. Andre Agassi made a surprise run, and it looked like the aging star might pull off a miracle before he lost to Roger Federer in the final. I had never photographed Agassi before, and I found him to be a powerful presence. No wonder the fans love him. I FIRST COVERED THE U.S. OPEN in the early 1960s, when it was played on the grass courts at Forest Hills in Queens. In '63 I took a picture from the top of the stadium, and I wanted to get the same sweeping view of the Open's new home, the National Tennis Center in Flushing Meadows. I used the same panoramic lens and camera, and the shots from the top of Arthur Ashe Stadium show how big the Open has become (pages 220–21). So do the aerial shots of the complex I took during a ride on the MetLife blimp. AS BEAUTIFUL AS THE TENNIS AERIALS ARE, my prize of the year came a few days later, from high above Yankee Stadium. Madison Square Garden and Yankee Stadium are where I grew up as a young photographer, and my entire career I'd wanted to get an aerial shot of the House That Ruth Built. This time I got a ride in the FUJIFILM BLIMP, right before dusk. Talk about magic hour. In that light, with the city going dark and the ballpark all lit up, the stadium looked like a jewel (pages 234–35). You couldn't miss. I'd anticipated that photograph for more than 40 years, and it was worth the wait. I WAS SO HAPPY WITH THOSE AERIALS that I went back up in the daytime (pages 236–37), and then I turned my attention to the Yankees' series against the Boston Red Sox. The two old rivals were locked in a pennant race, and I saw a duel between two pitchers who couldn't be more different. New York's Randy Johnson (page 249) is all power, while Boston's Tim Wakefield barely sweats as he tosses his knuckleballs (page 247). I liked that contrast in styles. Speaking of style, Red Sox centerfielder Johnny Damon was my subject of choice that weekend. He looked nothing like the other ballplayers I'd shot over the years, and even though he was in enemy territory he was great with the fans in the Bronx (page 244). He signed autographs for every kid, whether it was a Red Sox or Yankees fan. Maybe he knew he'd be playing for the home team the next season. DAMON CERTAINLY LOOKED DIFFERENT from the mostly crew-cut players I knew when I was younger. Yankee Stadium has changed, too, as you can see from the wide-angle shot I took from the stands behind home plate (page 241). I snapped a picture in the exact same spot during the 1961 World Series (page 240). My career had taken me far and wide since, but I was right back home again.

U.S. OPEN
ARTHUR ASHE STADIUM,
FLUSHING MEADOWS,
NEW YORK
SEPTEMBER 4–9, 2005

ANDRE AGASSI
ANDRE AGASSI VS. XAVIER MALISSE
SEPTEMBER 5, 2005

THE USTA NATIONAL TENNIS
CENTER FROM THE METLIFE BLIMP
U.S. Open
Arthur Ashe Stadium, Flushing Meadows,
New York, September 7, 2005

ARTHUR ASHE STADIUM AT DUSK
U.S. OPEN
FLUSHING MEADOWS, NEW YORK
SEPTEMBER 7, 2005

SEPTEMBER

OPPOSITE AND ABOVE:
ANDRE AGASSI
ANDRE AGASSI VS. XAVIER MALISSE
U.S. OPEN
ARTHUR ASHE STADIUM, FLUSHING MEADOWS,
NEW YORK, SEPTEMBER 5, 2005

PAGES: 224–25
U.S. NATIONAL CHAMPIONSHIPS
(BECAME THE U.S. OPEN)
THE WESTSIDE TENNIS CLUB
FOREST HILLS, NEW YORK
SEPTEMBER 1963

SEPTEMBER

SEPTEMBER

SEPTEMBER

YANKEE STADIUM
New York Yankees vs.
Tampa Bay Devil Rays
Bronx, New York
September 6, 2005

AT DUSK FROM THE FUJIFILM BLIMP

YANKEE STADIUM FROM THE
FUJIFILM BLIMP
New York Yankees vs. Boston Red Sox
Bronx, New York, September 10, 2005

SEPTEMBER

ABOVE AND OPPOSITE:
YANKEE STADIUM FROM THE
FUJIFILM BLIMP
New York Yankees vs. Tampa Bay Devil Rays
Bronx, New York, September 6, 2005

PAGES 240–41:
YANKEE STADIUM
Cincinnati Reds vs. New York Yankees
World Series Game 1
Bronx, New York, October 4, 1961

SEPTEMBER

SEPTEMBER

SEPTEMBER

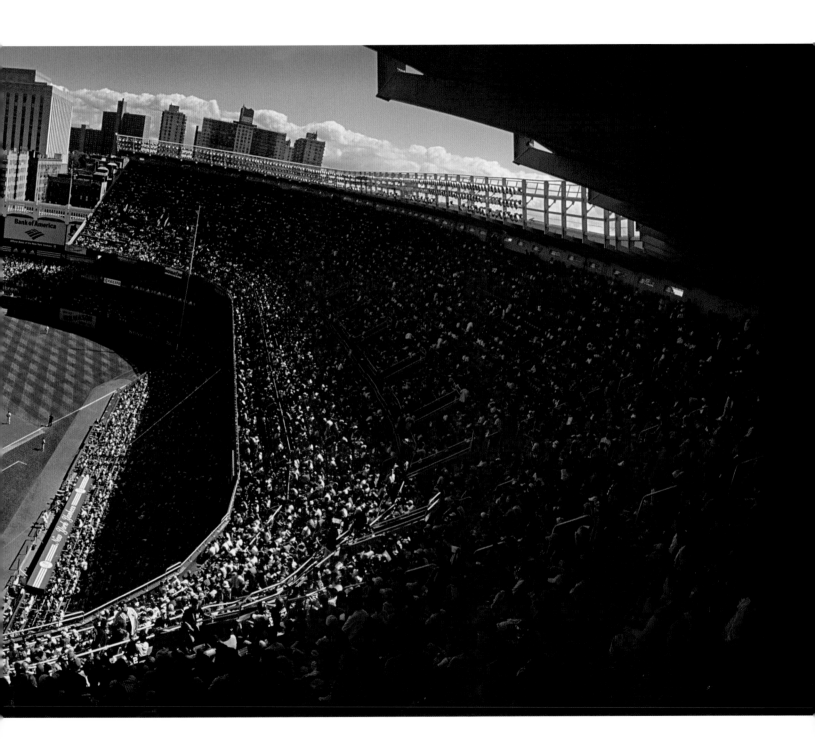

PAGES 242–43
YANKEE STADIUM

AND LEFT:
RED SOX'S JOHNNY DAMON
NEW YORK YANKEES VS. BOSTON RED SOX
YANKEE STADIUM
BRONX, NEW YORK, SEPTEMBER 11, 2005

LEFT:
NEW YORK YANKEES'
DEREK JETER

AND OPPOSITE:
BOSTON RED SOX'S
TIM WAKEFIELD
New York Yankees vs.
Boston Red Sox
Yankee Stadium,
Bronx, New York
September 11, 2005

SEPTEMBER

PAGE 248:
BOSTON RED SOX'S MANNY RAMIREZ

PAGE 249 AND LEFT:
NEW YORK YANKEES'
RANDY JOHNSON

PAGE 252:
NEW YORK YANKEES' MANAGER
JOE TORRE RELIEVES TOM GORDON

PAGE 253:
NEW YORK YANKEES' CLOSER
MARIANO RIVERA

New York Yankees vs. Boston Red Sox
Yankee Stadium, Bronx, New York
September 11, 2005

SEPTEMBER

OCTOBER

I WANTED THE PHOTOGRAPHS I took during the year to be fresh and original, not simply updates of things I'd taken before. But on a few occasions I was eager to duplicate an image from my archives. The month of October began and ended with two such moments. WHEN THE NATIONAL HOCKEY LEAGUE returned to the ice after a yearlong labor dispute, I shot the Montreal Canadiens and New York Rangers at Madison Square Garden. The Canadiens are the Yankees of hockey, and they've won more championships than anyone else. In the late 1950s and early 1960s I shot the Rangers and Canadiens from the cheap seats high up in the old Madison Square Garden (page 260). I wanted to shoot from the same angle in the new Garden, and in the process show how the sport had evolved (page 261). The players are much bigger. Everyone wears a helmet; in my shot from the '50s, even the goalie doesn't have a mask. And, like so much else in sports today, the ice is now essentially a billboard, advertising everything from hot dogs to cell phones. The only thing that hasn't changed is that classic Canadiens logo. I ENDED THE MONTH AT THE WORLD SERIES in Houston, where the Chicago White Sox finished off a sweep of the Astros. I asked for and was granted a photo position near the third base dugout. It was a perfect spot from which to replicate a picture I took in 1963 of an ecstatic Sandy Koufax leaping off the pitcher's mound after the Dodgers swept the Yankees (page 302). I love pictures that don't need a caption, and all the information the viewer needs is in that Koufax shot. The scoreboard and Koufax's smile tell the whole story. I GOT REALLY LUCKY, and everything fell into place in Houston:

The White Sox swept, and after the final out, closer Bobby Jenks turned directly toward me and leaped in front of the scoreboard. I knew right away that I had my shot. (That photo position also allowed me to get a few shots of former president George H.W. Bush and his wife, Barbara, who are big Astros fans and were seated behind home plate.) It was a historic moment for Chicago fans—their first title since 1917—and a very satisfying moment for me. BEFORE THE WORLD SERIES I did what I had done so often during my *SI* days: I spent a football weekend in Dallas. First, I went to the Texas vs. Oklahoma game in the Cotton Bowl. To me, Texas vs. Oklahoma *is* college football. The fans are loud and passionate, and with half the stands a sea of Longhorns orange and the other half awash in Sooners red, there's no more colorful background in sports. I also always considered it a lucky game for me. My first cover assignment for the magazine was to shoot Texas running back Jimmy Saxton in 1961. Though I didn't know it at the time, I again got lucky. On this visit I got to shoot the hero of the college football season: Texas quarterback Vince Young, who would lead the Longhorns to the national championship. THE NEXT DAY I WAS AT TEXAS STADIUM when the Philadelphia Eagles played the Dallas Cowboys. The Cowboys won, but I have to confess I spent a lot of time shooting the other famous team in the stadium, the Dallas Cowboys Cheerleaders. They bring some of the fun and color of college football to the pro game. BEFORE THE MONTH WAS OVER I read in the newspaper that there would be a sumo wrestling event at Madison Square Garden, and I knew I had to go. Sumo is a novelty in this country, and there's something humorous about those pictures. I was glad to add a few lighter moments to my collection of photographs.

NHL HOCKEY
New York Rangers vs.
Montreal Canadiens
Madison Square Garden,
New York, New York
October 6, 2005

ABOVE AND OPPOSITE:
MONTREAL CANADIENS
NHL Hockey
New York Rangers vs. Montreal Canadiens
Madison Square Garden, New York,
New York, October 6, 2005

OPPOSITE:
NEW YORK RANGERS VS.
MONTREAL CANADIENS
THE OLD MADISON SQUARE GARDEN,
NEW YORK, NEW YORK, OCTOBER 1959

ABOVE AND PAGES 262–63:
NEW YORK RANGERS VS.
MONTREAL CANADIENS
MADISON SQUARE GARDEN, NEW YORK,
NEW YORK, OCTOBER 6, 2005

TEXAS VS. OKLAHOMA

THE COTTON BOWL,
DALLAS, TEXAS
OCTOBER 8, 2005

TEXAS QUARTERBACK
VINCE YOUNG (#10)
THE TEXAS LONGHORNS ON OFFENSE
Texas vs. Oklahoma
The Cotton Bowl, Dallas, Texas
October 8, 2005

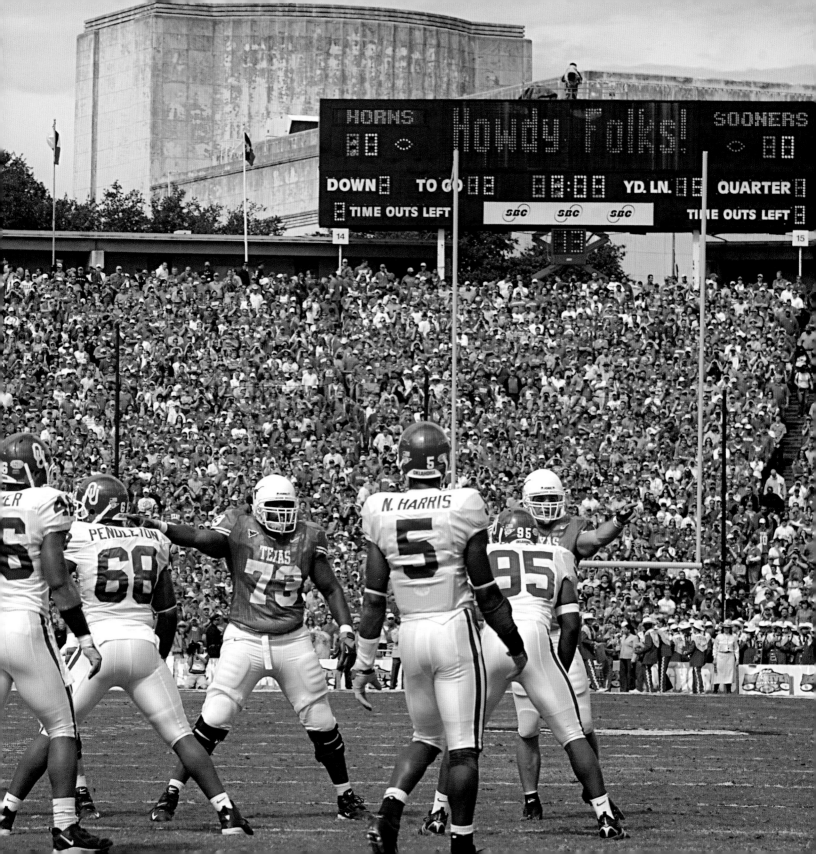

RIGHT
THE TEXAS POMS
TEXAS VS. OKLAHOMA
THE COTTON BOWL, DALLAS, TEXAS
OCTOBER 8, 2005

PAGES 270–71:
THE LONGHORNS DANCE SQUAD
AT HALFTIME
TEXAS VS. NAVY
THE COTTON BOWL, DALLAS, TEXAS
JANUARY 1, 1964

OCTOBER

OCTOBER

LONGHORNS FANS
Texas vs. Arkansas
Fayetteville, Arkansas
October 22, 1961

LONGHORNS FANS
Texas vs. Oklahoma
The Cotton Bowl, Dallas, Texas
October 8, 2005

TEXAS QUARTERBACK
VINCE YOUNG (#10)
Texas vs. Oklahoma
The Cotton Bowl, Dallas, Texas
October 8, 2005

OPPOSITE AND ABOVE:
VINCE YOUNG (#10)
TEXAS VS. OKLAHOMA
THE COTTON BOWL, DALLAS, TEXAS
OCTOBER 8, 2005

BELOW:
THE LONGHORNS' VICTORIOUS
HEAD COACH DARRELL ROYAL
(WHITE SHIRT WITH TIE)
Texas vs. Oklahoma
The Cotton Bowl, Dallas, Texas
October 12, 1963

OPPOSITE:
THE LONGHORNS' VICTORIOUS
HEAD COACH MAC BROWN
Texas vs. Oklahoma
The Cotton Bowl, Dallas, Texas
October 8, 2005

OCTOBER

NFL FOOTBALL
DALLAS COWBOYS VS.
PHILADELPHIA EAGLES
TEXAS STADIUM, IRVING, TEXAS
OCTOBER 9, 2005

THE DALLAS COWBOY CHEERLEADERS

OCTOBER

THE COWBOYS' DEFENSE
DALLAS COWBOYS VS. PHILADELPHIA EAGLES
NFL FOOTBALL
TEXAS STADIUM, IRVING, TEXAS
OCTOBER 9, 2005

OPPOSITE:
COWBOYS' QUARTERBACK
DREW BLEDSOE (#11) AND EAGLES'
JEVON KEARSE (#93)

AND ABOVE:
COWBOYS' HEAD COACH
BILL PARCELLS
DALLAS COWBOYS VS. PHILADELPHIA EAGLES
NFL FOOTBALL
TEXAS STADIUM, IRVING, TEXAS
OCTOBER 9, 2005

COWBOYS' MIKE PATTERSON (#98)
AND EAGLES' DONOVAN MCNABB
Dallas Cowboys vs. Philadelphia Eagles
NFL Football
Texas Stadium, Irving, Texas
October 9, 2005

SUMO WRESTLING
Madison Square Garden,
New York, New York
October 22, 2005

MITSHUHIKO FUKAO (JAPAN) VS.
PETAR STOYANOV (BULGARIA)

OCTOBER

LEFT:
MITSHUHIKO FUKAO

AND OPPOSITE:
PETAR STOYANOV VS.
MITSHUHIKO FUKAO
SUMO WRESTLING
MADISON SQUARE GARDEN, NEW YORK,
NEW YORK, OCTOBER 22, 2005

OCTOBER

WORLD SERIES
Chicago White Sox vs.
Houston Astros
Minute Maid Park,
Houston, Texas
October 25–26, 2005

ASTROS' FAN FORMER PRESIDENT
GEORGE H.W. BUSH

OCTOBER

THE 13TH INNING OF THE
LONGEST GAME IN
WORLD SERIES HISTORY:
ASTROS' PITCHER CHAD QUALLS
Chicago White Sox vs. Houston Astros
World Series — Game 3
Minute Maid Park, Houston, Texas
October 25, 2005

ABOVE:
NEW YORK YANKEES VS.
MILWAUKEE BRAVES
WORLD SERIES
YANKEE STADIUM, BRONX, NEW YORK
OCTOBER 1958

RIGHT:
CHICAGO WHITE SOX VS.
HOUSTON ASTROS
WORLD SERIES — GAME 4
MINUTE MAID PARK, HOUSTON, TEXAS
OCTOBER 26, 2005

OCTOBER

MinuteMaid
Park

AmegyBank of Texas   Continental Airlines   AIM INVESTMENTS

Methodist
The Methodist
Hospital

new ballgame
HOUSTON CHRONICLE

WHITE SOX		2005 WS STATS				ASTROS			2B
22 Podsednik	LF					7 Biggio			2B
15 Iguchi	2B	RF Dye				1 Taveras			CF
23 Dye	RF	AVG .333				17 Berkman			LF
14 Konerko	1B					14 Ensberg			3B
12 Pierzynski	C					26 Lamb			1B
33 Rowand	CF					16 Lane			RF
24 Crede	3B					11 Ausmus			C
5 Uribe	SS					26 Everett			SS
34 Garcia	P					41 Backe			P

JERMAINE DYE
2005 POSTSEASON (11 GAMES)
AVG .268   HR 1   RBI 5

1 2 3 4 5 6 7 8 9 10   R H E LOB   BALL STRIKE OUT

	1 2 3 4 5 6 7 8 9 10	R	H	E	LOB
WHITE SOX	0 0 0 0	0	0	0	0
ASTROS	0 0 0 0	0	0	0	0

BALL STRIKE OUT
3 1 2

FOLEY'S   7:46   LYONDELL   mbna

BORDEN   373   JPMorganChase   LAND MARK CHEVROLET   H-E-B   AMERIQUEST MORTGAGE COMPANY

ASTROS' PITCHER BRANDON BACKE
AND WHITE SOX'S BATTER
JERMAINE DYE;
AJ PIERZYNSKI IN THE BATTER'S BOX
Chicago White Sox vs. Houston Astros
World Series—Game 4
Minute Maid Park, Houston, Texas
October 26, 2005

ABOVE:
FANS CELEBRATE WHITE SOX'S
SWEEP OF THE SERIES

AND OPPOSITE:
DISAPPOINTED FANS—FORMER
PRESIDENT GEORGE H.W. BUSH
AND BARBARA BUSH
CHICAGO WHITE SOX VS. HOUSTON ASTROS
WORLD SERIES—GAME 4
MINUTE MAID PARK, HOUSTON, TEXAS
OCTOBER 26, 2005

BELOW:
SANDY KOUFAX CELEBRATES
SWEEP OF THE YANKEES
NEW YORK YANKEES VS. L.A. DODGERS
WORLD SERIES—GAME 4
DODGER STADIUM, LOS ANGELES, CALIFORNIA
OCTOBER 6, 1963

OPPOSITE:
BOBBIE JENKS CELEBRATES
SWEEP OF THE ASTROS
CHICAGO WHITE SOX VS. HOUSTON ASTROS
WORLD SERIES—GAME 4
MINUTE MAID PARK, HOUSTON, TEXAS
OCTOBER 26, 2005

OCTOBER

NOVEMBER

IT TAKES GOOD FORTUNE to get a great picture, and when the calendar turned to November, the fantastic luck I'd been having all year seemed to fade. I love boxing, and I had planned to go to Las Vegas for the Hasim Rahman–Vitali Klitschko heavyweight title fight. Alas, Klitschko pulled out with an injury a week before the bout, and I lost my chance to see a big-time championship fight. I also had rotten luck at the New York Marathon. My plan was to shoot the start of the world's largest marathon from a helicopter; there's nothing like the sight of thousands of runners charging across the Verrazano-Narrows Bridge. But on the morning of the race the whole city was fogged in, and the helicopter couldn't land to pick me up, much less fly over Staten Island and Brooklyn. Suddenly, with no title fight and no marathon, there were no pictures to take in November. SOMETIMES BEING A PHOTOGRAPHER is like being a quarterback—when things don't work out as planned, you call an audible. I started hunting for fun events to shoot, and I found the perfect one: pee-wee football. I had the ideal subjects in mind, too. My nine-year-old grandson Joey, who lives in Boca Raton, Florida, is a running back for the Boca Jets. His sister Taylor, who's seven, is a cheerleader for the team. So I flew down to do what any proud grandfather loves to do— spend time with my daughter, Jodi, and my two favorite subjects. As a bonus, I got some terrific pictures. IT'S EASY TO FORGET THAT THE PRO STARS WE WATCH on Sundays weren't always larger than life. They started out wearing oversized helmets and tossing junior-sized footballs just like Joey and his friends. Well, it's easy for adults to forget.

To the kids, this park in Florida might as well have been Green Bay's Frozen Tundra. It was great fun to watch them act out their gridiron dreams. Who knows, maybe I'll be shooting one of the Boca Jets in a much larger stadium some day. LIKE, SAY, GIANTS STADIUM IN NEW JERSEY, where I saw the New York Giants and Minnesota Vikings square off the following day. The Giants lost, but I was concerned with photographing one of the NFL's rising stars, New York's Eli Manning. The Manning family is to quarterbacking what the Bushes are to politics. Eli's brother Peyton stars for the Indianapolis Colts, and I photographed their father, Archie, when he was a college standout at Mississippi. That wasn't the only reason the game brought me back to my youth. Giants games were my photography training ground in the 1950s and '60s, and one of my favorite subjects back then was star running back Frank Gifford. You looked for him first on every play. As luck would have it Frank was there to watch his old team play the Vikings, and he was the first person I saw when I walked onto the field. It was great to see a new generation of stars on the field, and to reconnect with an old friend on the sidelines. WHEN I SHOT THE SUMO EVENT at Madison Square Garden in October, my friend and former *SI* colleague Frank Deford teased me, saying I was searching for "big events," because I was having so much fun on my tour. He was right. November was supposed to mark the end of the Senior Citizen Tour; *Sports Illustrated* would be publishing my photo essay the week after the Giants–Vikings game, and I hadn't scheduled any more shoots. But as I left Giants Stadium, I realized I didn't want my fantastic year to be a month short. I immediately checked the sports calendar for December.

PEE WEE FOOTBALL
THE BOCA JETS VS. PPO BENGALS
BOCA RATON, FLORIDA
NOVEMBER 12, 2005

PAGE 308:
BOCA JETS' JOEY OSBORNE (#33)

PAGE 309:
BOCA JETS' CHEERLEADERS,
TAYLOR OSBORNE (2ND FROM RIGHT)

NOVEMBER

BOCA JETS CELEBRATE VICTORY
The Boca Jets vs. PPO Bengals
Pee Wee Football
Boca Raton, Florida
November 12, 2005

NOVEMBER

DEJECTION ON THE PPO BENGALS BENCH
The Boca Jets vs. PPO Bengals
Pee Wee Football
Boca Raton, Florida
November 12, 2005

NFL FOOTBALL
New York Giants vs.
Minnesota Vikings
Giants Stadium,
The Meadowlands
East Rutherford,
New Jersey
November 13, 2005

New York Giants Quarterback
Eli Manning (#10)

NOVEMBER

OPPOSITE:
NEW YORK GIANTS RUNNING BACK
TIKI BARBER (#21)
NEW YORK GIANTS VS. MINNESOTA VIKINGS
NFL FOOTBALL
GIANTS STADIUM, THE MEADOWLANDS
EAST RUTHERFORD, NEW JERSEY
NOVEMBER 13, 2005

ABOVE:
NEW YORK GIANTS' HALFBACK
FRANK GIFFORD (#16)
NEW YORK GIANTS VS. WASHINGTON REDSKINS
NFL FOOTBALL
YANKEE STADIUM, BRONX, NEW YORK
NOVEMBER 29, 1959

DECEMBER

ONE EVENT JUMPED out when I was planning the final month of my sports odyssey: USC vs. UCLA at the Los Angeles Coliseum. I love shooting at the Coliseum, which has been my favorite stadium since I first set foot in it in 1961. It's beautiful and full of history. Plus, the undefeated Trojans seemed to be rolling toward a third straight national championship. They crushed the Bruins, 66–19, guaranteeing that they'd play in the Bowl Championship Series title game. USC running back Reggie Bush (pages 324–25) ran for 260 yards and a week later won the Heisman Trophy. MAYBE I JINXED THE TROJANS; Texas, not USC, ended up as the national champ. No matter. I got some wonderful pictures, and being in L.A. put me in perfect position for another plum assignment. Sylvester Stallone and I have been friends since 1978 when I took pictures for him on the set of *Rocky II,* and we've worked together on *Rocky III* and several of his other movies. When I heard that he'd be filming the fight scenes for *Rocky Balboa,* a new Rocky film, at the Mandalay Bay in Las Vegas the day after the USC–UCLA game, I called him up. He invited me to the set. ROCKY'S OPPONENT IN THE FILM is played by Antonio Tarver, the reigning light-heavyweight champion of the world. Stallone, who stars and directs, looked great—you'd never guess that he's 60 years old—and in the ring he and Tarver went at it hard. Sly is a stickler for detail. The referee was a real referee, the ringside judges were real Las Vegas judges, and I shot the scene through the ropes, as if it were a real fight being featured in *Sports Illustrated.* I came away with two of the best boxing action pictures I've ever taken (pages 326–27).

Of course, I still don't know how the fight turned out. Stallone, not wanting to give away the movie's ending, shot two versions of the scene. When I see it in the theater, I'll be on the edge of my seat like everyone else. A WEEK LATER I WENT TO BOSTON to photograph another favorite sport, women's figure skating. It was an exhibition at Boston University, and it featured the three top U.S. skaters: Michelle Kwan, Sasha Cohen, and Emily Hughes. I shot from the catwalk directly above the ice, and just before the event ended I got a truly memorable shot. At the close of her final program Cohen, who won a silver medal at the Turin Olympics two months later, lay down on the ice, looked up at me, and flashed a beautiful smile. I knew right away that I had a fantastic image, one of my best of the year. THAT WAS IT, MY FINAL SHOOT OF THE YEAR. It was sort of sad, and probably I was looking for a way to extend things. Reading the sports pages on the train ride home from Boston to New York, I noticed that the Indianapolis Colts were undefeated and closing in on the 1972 Miami Dolphins' 17–0 record. They were playing at home the following Sunday—in the climate-controlled RCA Dome, the best way to see a December game. So I decided to head for Indianapolis. If the Colts were going to make history, I wanted to be there. WHEN I LANDED IN INDY the Colts were 13–0. When I left they were 13–1, having lost to the San Diego Chargers, and when they lost in the playoffs a few weeks later I wondered if the Neil Leifer jinx had struck again. But I couldn't be disappointed. Because the Chargers chased Peyton Manning all over the field, I got some really good action pictures of the Colts quarterback. As a photographer, not just a fan, my year had ended on a high note. I can always root for the Colts in 2006.

USC VS. UCLA
THE LOS ANGELES MEMORIAL COLISEUM
LOS ANGELES, CALIFORNIA
DECEMBER 3, 2005

PAGE 320:
THE USC TROJANS FANS

PAGE 321:
THE USC TROJANS ENTER
THE COLISEUM

DECEMBER

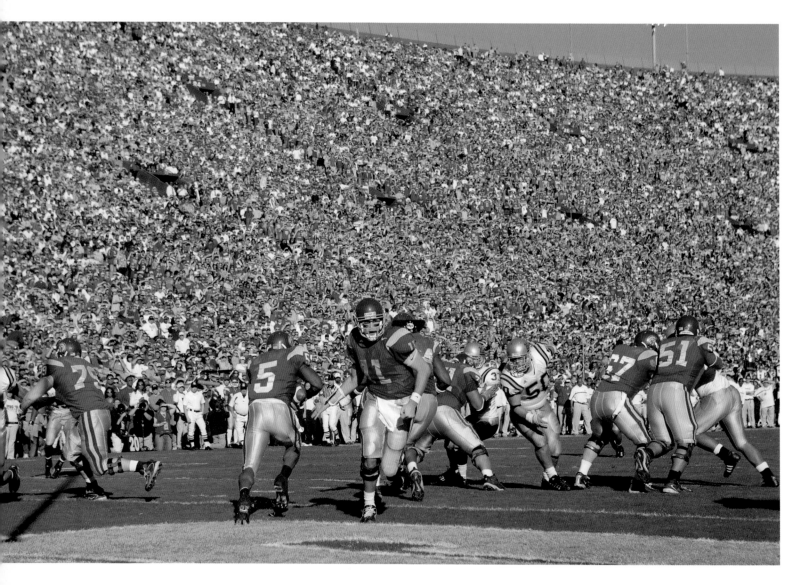

ABOVE:
THE TROJANS' REGGIE BUSH (#5)
AND MATT LEINART (#11)

AND OPPOSITE:
HEISMAN TROPHY WINNER (2004)
MATT LEINART ROLLS OUT TO PASS
USC vs. UCLA
THE LOS ANGELES MEMORIAL COLISEUM
LOS ANGELES, CALIFORNIA
DECEMBER 3, 2005

DECEMBER

HEISMAN TROPHY WINNER (2005)
REGGIE BUSH (#5) OFF AND RUNNING
USC vs. UCLA
The Los Angeles Memorial Coliseum
Los Angeles, California
December 3, 2005

DECEMBER

SYLVESTER STALLONE
AND
ANTONIO TARVER
On the set of *Rocky Balboa*
Mandalay Bay Arena,
Las Vegas, Nevada
December 4–6, 2005

PAGES 328–329:
SYLVESTER STALLONE AND
ANTONIO TARVER

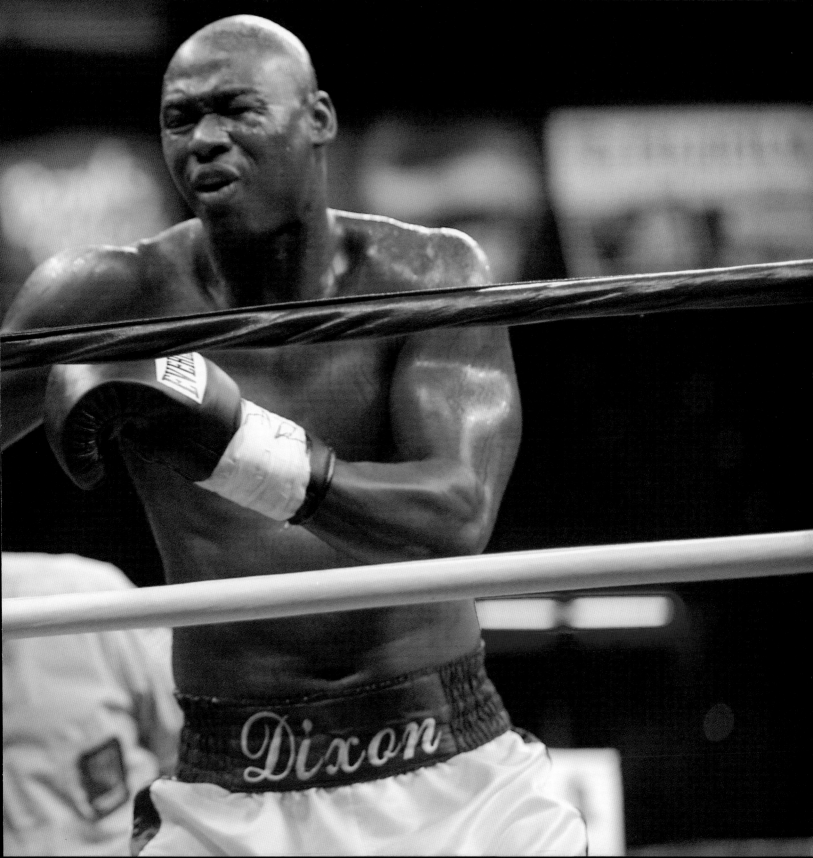

THE U.S. FIGURE SKATING CHALLENGE

AGGANIS ARENA AT BOSTON
UNIVERSITY
BOSTON, MASSACHUSETTS
DECEMBER 11, 2005

LEFT:
SASHA COHEN

PAGE 332–333:
MICHELLE KWAN

PAGE 334:
SASHA COHEN

PAGE 335:
EMILY HUGHES

NFL FOOTBALL
SAN DIEGO CHARGERS VS.
INDIANAPOLIS COLTS
RCA DOME,
INDIANAPOLIS, INDIANA
DECEMBER 18, 2005

COLTS' QUARTERBACK
PEYTON MANNING (#18)

DECEMBER

AND BELOW:
PEYTON MANNING (#18) AND
THE COLTS' OFFENSE
San Diego Chargers vs. Indianapolis Colts
NFL Football
RCA Dome, Indianapolis, Indiana
December 18, 2005

LEFT:
PEYTON MANNING ON
THE COLTS' BENCH

AND PAGE 342:
QUARTERBACK PEYTON MANNING
IN THE POCKET
SAN DIEGO CHARGERS VS. INDIANAPOLIS COLTS
NFL CHAMPIONSHIP GAME
RCA DOME, INDIANAPOLIS, INDIANA
DECEMBER 18, 2005

PAGE 343:
BALTIMORE COLTS' QUARTERBACK
JOHNNY UNITAS (#19)
NEW YORK GIANTS VS. BALTIMORE COLTS
NFL CHAMPIONSHIP GAME
MEMORIAL STADIUM, BALTIMORE, MARYLAND
DECEMBER 27, 1959

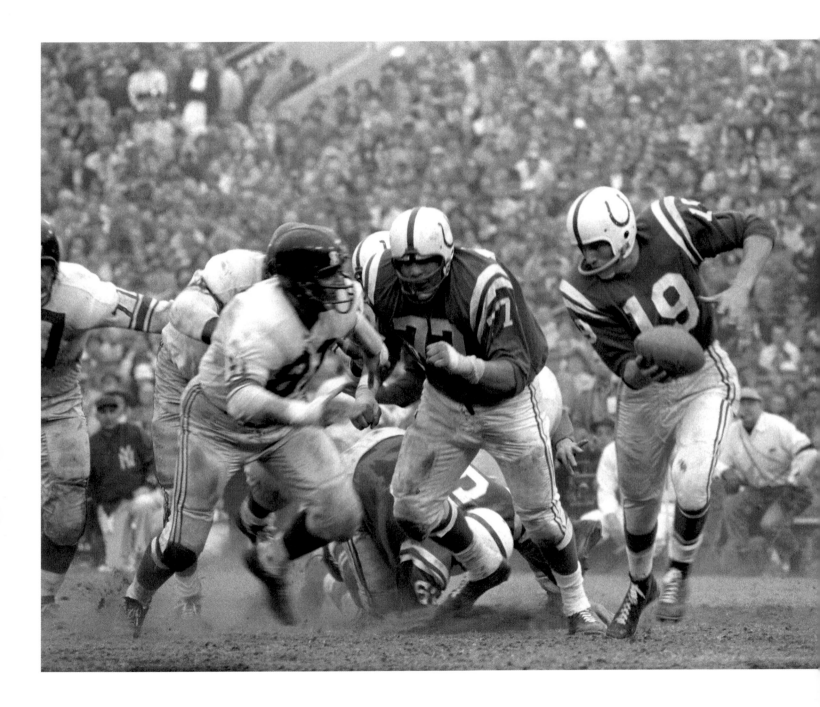

LEFT:
COLTS' QUARTERBACK PEYTON
MANNING IN TROUBLE

AND ABOVE:
TONY DUNGY, HEAD COACH
OF THE COLTS
San Diego Chargers vs. Indianapolis Colts
NFL Football
RCA Dome, Indianapolis, Indiana
December 18, 2005

345

ACKNOWLEDGMENTS

I HAVE DEDICATED THIS BOOK to three very special people: Terry McDonell, Frank Deford and Corey Leifer. WITHOUT *Sports Illustrated*'s Managing Editor Terry McDonell the Senior Citizen Tour would have never happened. I will forever be grateful to him for the confidence he had in me and for saying yes to my wild idea. FRANK DEFORD has been both a great friend and a great collaborator for almost forty years. I am honored that he would write the introduction to my book, and it was terrific fun to have him along for parts of my Tour. It was just like old times. MY SON COREY assisted me at eleven of my Tour stops. It was father-son bonding at its very best. Neither of us will ever forget 2005. When Corey was unable to join me, my fiancée, Randye Stein, more than ably filled his shoes. One of them wins "assistant of the year"; I'm just not saying which one. I ALSO MUST THANK ANDY CARD, President Bush's former White House chief of staff, for personally making sure that my dream to go to the Opening Day baseball game with the president became a reality. I thank President Bush for saying yes to my request. ABBEVILLE PRESS published *The Best of Leifer* in 2001, and once again I am very fortunate to have teamed up with Bob Abrams, Susan Costello, and Louise Kurtz of Abbeville. Patricia Fabricant who designed this book has done a first-class job. MY BROTHER HOWIE worked very long days, weeks, and months putting the pictures for this book in order. Ditto for my assistant Joan Fazekas. *Sports Illustrated*'s Director of Photography Steve Fine encouraged and supported me all year. Most importantly, he gave me David Bergman as my "digital" tutor. Without David I would not have survived the year. Steve Cannella shaped my words into readable text. PHOTOGRAPHERS ALWAYS COMPLAIN that they don't get enough space for their pictures; I've never heard one say a book or magazine piece should have more words. But when I sat down to write this page I realized that the 300 words I was allotted would never be enough to thank all the photographers, assistants, editors, publicists, and others who helped make the Senior Citizen Tour so enjoyable and successful. Even if I can't mention them all by name, I hope all those people understand how grateful I am.

—NEIL LEIFER

April 2006

INDEX

347